Blue **Peter**
World of Music

Rob Kearsley Bullen • Michael Cox
With special thanks to The BBC Philharmonic Orchestra, Steve Hocking,
Edwina Wolstencroft, Martin Maris and Kate Walker

Cartoons by Mark Oliver

Contents

Acknowledgements

Cartoons: P8,9,11,23,26,28,30,33,41,44,45,47,55,56 © Mark Oliver

Photographs:

Photographs of members of the BBC Philharmonic Orchestra © Alan Hamer and thanks to the BBC Philharmonic Orchestra

P9   Australian Aborigine didgeridoo player © Paul A. Saunders/CORBIS

P10 Pianist Thelonious Monk © Ted Williams/CORBIS

P12 Balinese Gamelan musician playing gongs © ROBERT HARDING

P13 Indonesian Gamelan Orchestra © ROBERT HARDING

P17 Photographs of young musicians, p.17, 24, 49 © The National Youth Orchestra

P19 Belly dancer © Israel Talby/ROBERT HARDING

P24 Tuba © AKG Photo/Erik Bohr

P25 Louis Armstrong © Bettmann/CORBIS

P31 Japanese Koto Player © Nigel Blythe/ROBERT HARDING

P31 Musician playing shakuhachi © Jeremy Hoare/LIFE FILE

P31 Taiko drummer © Jon Burbank/HUTCHINSON LIBRARY

P38 Yamaha grand piano courtesy of Yamaha

P39 Field with sheep © eye ubiquitous

P40 Lumbee women © Lourdes Grobet/LINK

P45 Bourbon St, New Orleans © C. Bowman/ROBERT HARDING

P48 African marimbas © Julia Baker

P51 Nasser Shamma © Al Hayat

P58 The east end of the River Thames © eye ubiquitous

P60 Dhol player © S. Kay/LIFE FILE

Published by BBC Educational Publishing,
BBC White City,
201 Wood Lane, London W12 7TS

First published 2001

© Rob Kearsley Bullen, Michael Cox/BBC Worldwide (Educational Publishing), 2001

Printed by Sterling Press

Book only ISBN 0 563 54203 9   CD only ISBN 0 563 54200 4   Book and CD pack ISBN 0 563 542772

To place an order, please telephone Customer Services on 0870 830 8000 (Monday – Friday, 0800-1800) or write to BBC Educational Publishing, P.O. Box 234, Wetherby, West Yorkshire, LS23 7EU

Visit the BBC Education website at: www.bbc.co.uk/schools

Introduction

Welcome to the Blue Peter World of Music. You'll find every type of music here, played on everything from the violin to the didgeridoo, all of it music that you'll hear on Blue Peter if you watch regularly. We hope that you'll find some favourite pieces and, better still, some pieces that you've never heard before that may become your favourites!

On the CD that accompanies this book, you can listen to the wide variety of different sounds, and in the book you can read about who composed them, what they are about, which instruments are played on them and how they fit into the world of music.

The music on the CD and the sections in the book are divided into seven 'Rooms', each with a different theme. Each room features music from different times in history and different places around the world, but the music in each one helps to create the mood of the room. The music in the dance room will make you want to jump around and the Crash! Bang! Room is LOUD!

As well as reading about each track that's on the CD, you can find out about the instruments of the orchestra, the background to different tunes and the lives of the people who wrote them. You'll also discover some weird and wonderful facts about music and musicians, try out some musical styles and, in true Blue Peter style, you can have a go at making simple musical instruments yourself.

We hope that you'll enjoy exploring our World of Music.

Rhythm Room

Welcome to the Rhythm Room. The tunes you'll hear in this area have all got strong or lively rhythms which are extremely infectious.

These are rhythms that get beneath your skin, set your toes tapping and your fingers snapping. Perhaps it's because they are like the rhythms that are inside all of us, such as the beat of your heart, the rise and fall of your breathing, and the throbbing of your pulse.

The word rhythm comes from an Ancient Greek word which means 'flow'. In music, the rhythm section musicians play the background flow, or sound pattern, while all the others tell the 'story' by playing the main tune or melody. Some people, such as the Javanese 'gamelan' musicians on track 8 (see pages 12-13), reckon music isn't music if it hasn't got a regular, rhythmic beat.

Where's the beat?

Once, a Canadian musician played some solo piano music to a group of Javanese gamelan musicians (see page 13). They asked him where the beat was! They told him that music without a beat is like a bird with a broken wing. Gamelan musicians often play lots of different rhythms at the same time.

Tambourine

Maracas

Do-it-yourself shaker

Take two plastic drinking cups and put a few dried beans or some uncooked rice inside one of them. Seal the two cups together with sticky tape and shake!

CUBA

Track 3: Mambo, Leonard Bernstein

'Mambo' is a dance number from a musical show called 'West Side Story', by Leonard Bernstein. There are lots of Latin American (that's South American) percussion instruments (see right) to listen for. Here are some of them:

- maracas (sound like dried peas in a yoghurt pot)
- claves (two wooden sticks tapped together)
- cowbells (tinkle like a cow's bell)

But rhythm isn't just about percussion — the whole orchestra is a rhythm instrument in this piece. The musicians even have to shout in rhythm, too. Bernstein didn't make up the word 'Mambo', by the way. It's a real dance from Cuba, related to the Rumba and the Cha Cha, which are other rhythmic, Latin American dances.

Leonard Bernstein (1918–1990)

Leonard Bernstein came from Lawrence, Massachusetts in the USA. He conducted the New York Philharmonic Orchestra for twelve years. He wrote all kinds of music, including musical shows, such as 'West Side Story'. Bernstein also wrote books. One of them was called *The Joy of Music*. He must have changed his mind, because twelve years earlier he wrote a group of songs called 'I Hate Music'!

Michael Escreet

Playing pizzicato

Musicians often play the double bass with a bow, but most of 'Mambo' is played pizzicato (pronounced pit-see-KAH-toe). This means plucking the strings with your fingers. 'Mambo' is played very fast and Michael Escreet, of the BBC Philharmonic Orchestra, who played double bass on this track, says that plucking the heavy double bass strings can give players a blister on their finger.

Orchestral percussion instruments

Percussion instruments are ones you play by hitting, shaking or rattling. In an orchestra there are three groups of percussion instruments.

Timpani

Timpani (tuned drums) are the 'kettle drums' that you usually see at the back of the orchestra. They are huge, bowl-shaped metal drums, with a skin stretched across the top that is tuned by turning the 'taps' all around the edge. Listen for them under the tune of the 'Star Trek Theme' (Track 37) and at the start of 'Star Wars March' (Track 50).

Side drum

The **untuned percussion** group contains all kinds of things. One of the best-known is the side drum, or snare drum. It makes the 'rattly' sound at the start of the Blue Peter signature tune (Track 1) and all through the 'Radetzky March' (Track 6). You can hear the big bass drum (it's over a metre high) on lots of tracks: 'Mambo' (Track 3) and 'The Defeat of Napoleon' (Track 43). This group also has all the instruments made of wood or metal: wood blocks, claves, triangles, cymbals, gongs and cow bells.

Cow bell

Tuned percussion instruments include anything you can play a tune on with sticks or hammers, such as xylophones and marimbas (hear a marimba on Track 12, 'Sabre Dance' and Track 40, 'Denka', and see one on page 48); and the metal bar instruments: metallophone (Track 8, 'Kodakan'), glockenspiels (Track 50, halfway through the 'Star Wars March'), and vibraphone (Track 12, 'Sabre Dance', at the end). There are also tubular bells and other unusual things.

Julian Gregory is from the BBC Philharmonic's first violins. He says that 'Wild Bears' is one of the show-off pieces for the string section of the orchestra. They often play it as an encore at the end of a concert. It gives them a chance to show how fast they can play without going wrong.

Julian Gregory

Test your friends:

Can you name the composer of Ravel's 'Bolero'?

(You'll see the answer on page 39.)

Track 4: Wild Bears, Elgar

This piece of music took Edward Elgar, the composer, 40 years to write! Well, sort of. Young Edward and his brothers and sisters used to make up plays about a special world they'd invented.

When he was eleven, Edward wrote some tunes to go with one of their plays. Forty years later, he found one of his old books with the tunes in it and realised that they were really quite good. So he arranged them for full orchestra and called the finished set 'The Wand of Youth'. 'Wild Bears' is the last of the thirteen pieces in the set.

Sir Edward Elgar (1857–1934)

Elgar was born in Broadheath, near Worcester, England. One of the orchestras he conducted was called the Worcester County Lunatic Asylum Band! For most of his life, Elgar lived in Malvern. There's an Elgar Trail through the Malvern Hills (if you're ever around there, look for little brown signs with a violin on them).

Elgar was football crazy. Once he went to see Wolverhampton Wanderers play and later read a report on the game in the paper. The sports reporter wrote, 'He banged the leather for goal,' as part of the article. Elgar liked the rhythm of the words. He set one of the tunes he was working on for a piece called 'Caractacus' to the rhythm, as a joke. No-one's been heard chanting it on the football terraces yet, though!

Elgar's most famous piece is 'Pomp and Circumstance March no. 1'. Most people know it as 'Land of Hope and Glory', which is sung every year at the Last Night of the Proms. The Proms, or Promenade Concerts, make up a huge, two-month-long festival of music every year.

Aboriginal Australian playing a didgeridoo

Track 5:
Dingo Dance, Peter Thoms and Doug Coulter

OK, let's get this straight, dingoes don't dance. They are wild dogs that live in Australia. The aboriginal people of Australia sometimes train young dingoes as hunting dogs. Most aboriginal music is based on the sounds of the outback (the wild interior of Australia) and the animals that live there. 'Dingo Dance' is played on two didgeridoos and blocks of wood called 'clap sticks'. The main rhythm of the music is a good example of rhythm coming from a wind instrument, rather than percussion. The weird sound effects are made by blowing rapid blasts of air into the tube of the didgeridoo and humming at the same time (see right).

Track 6:
Radetzky March, Johann Strauss I

This famous tune was written by Johann Strauss I in 1848. It's meant to sound like military music, the sort of thing soldiers march along to (although this version on the CD is rather fast, so it's more like a run). You can hear the military drums and cymbals in the background.

Brain teaser

The 'Radetzky March' comes with a free tongue-twister! Radetzky (say rad-ETS-key) was in charge of the Austrian army when Strauss was alive, and he was very famous and popular. His full name was...

JOHANN JOSEPH WENZEL ANTON FRANZ KARL, GRAF RADETZKY VON RADETZ

– try saying that ten times quickly!

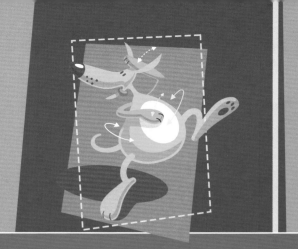

Do-it-yourself didgeridoo

Try this: rub your stomach with one hand and pat your head with the other. Tricky, eh? Now try this: breathe in through your nose and out through your mouth – at the same time. That's called circular breathing and you need to do it to play the didgeridoo.

Now use the air you're breathing out to 'blow a raspberry' down a big tube (a huge cardboard one, for instance), and sing at the same time. That's what you have to do to play a didgeridoo. You can only play one note on it – but no-one's going to notice, they'll be too busy watching your face turn purple!

Johann Strauss I (1804-1849)

The most confusing thing about Johann Strauss is that there are two of him! The Johann Baptist Strauss who composed the Radetzky March had a son, also called Johann Baptist Strauss. Johann I was going to be a bookbinder at first, but soon found that music suited him better. He wrote over 250 pieces of dance music — that's enough to fill about forty CDs — but the 'Radetzky March' is about the only one that still gets played. To make things more confusing, Johann II became a composer as well. He wrote famous waltzes, such as 'The Blue Danube', that are still popular.

Q. What do you get if you drop a piano down a coal mine?

A. A flat minor.

strange, but true

Traffic rhythms

Thelonious Monk had a brilliant sense of rhythm and loved to 'play' with everyday sounds.

He would dance in and out of the New York traffic as it slowed for stop lights. He enjoyed the rhythmic 'flow' of honking horns and roaring engines (and yelling drivers, perhaps!).

Thelonious Monk

Track 7: Straight No Chaser, Thelonious Monk

'Straight No Chaser' is a jazz tune written by Thelonious Monk. Lots of music fans and musicians know and love this tune. They've done all sorts of things with it: named their bands after it, named magazines after it, written song lyrics for it, named radio programmes after it… and they've improvised with it. (If you're not sure what that means, see the section on the page opposite.)

The drums, piano and bass provide the toe-tapping backing, and the trumpet and violin are the first to play the main tune 'idea'. Next, the violin grabs the tune and improvises with it for a while. Then the trumpet snatches it back and does its own thing. Finally, the violin jumps back in and repeats the main tune with a bit of help from the trumpet.

Thelonious Monk (1917–1982)

Thelonious Monk was a really famous American jazz pianist. He wrote stacks of brilliant tunes that are played by all sorts of musicians all over the world. Thelonious started playing the piano when he was five and got his first music jobs playing in churches and at parties. Eventually, he got to play with famous jazz musicians, such as Charlie Parker and Dizzy Gillespie. Finally, he got his own band.

At first, lots of people didn't know what to make of Thelonious. They thought he was a bit odd. He'd do strange things, like get up and have a little dance while the other musicians played their solos. He also seemed to have the biggest collection of weird and wonderful hats in the world. Every time he appeared at a concert or on a record cover, he'd be wearing a different, snazzy hat. Quite a few people were a bit scared of him, too. It may have been because, if someone asked him a really stupid question, he'd just ignore them completely.

When Thelonious wrote a new tune he didn't show his musicians the music or even tell them its title. He'd just play it to them on the piano, or hum it. He wanted them to get the 'feel' of it rather than be bogged down in written words and music.

Some people thought he lived in a world of his own, but this was probably because he was thinking about music all the time. One day, he was playing with his son outdoors when he had a brilliant idea for a tune. So he composed the whole thing there and then, sitting in his son's pedal car!

Thelonious reckoned he could create music any time, anywhere. One musician who visited found him composing jazz on his piano – with a radio on top, blasting out Country and Western music. Now, that's what you call good concentration!

strange, but true

Once, when Thelonious was walking down the street, a big dog rushed up and sank its teeth into his leg. Thelonious ignored it, just as he ignored the dumb questions people asked. He carried on walking down the street with the dog attached to his leg. This confused the dog who, in the end, simply let go of his leg and ran off.

What is improvising?

Imagine you're in a tricky situation – you've arrived hours late for school, for example. You've got to think of a good excuse on the spot. You just start inventing a story, and add good details to it as you go along. In other words, you take an idea then expand on it as the inspiration grabs you. That's more or less what improvising is about, and it's what's happening on tracks 7 and 16.

Track 8: Kodakan, Traditional

'Kodakan' isn't just the name of this piece. It's a style of playing that is used by Javanese gamelan groups (see the next page). Kodakan works like this: there's a tune, but it's split between two players. Each player has to play every other note. Imagine how difficult it is to get the timing right.

If you've got someone to work with, try this out for yourself. See Do-it-yourself Kodakan, below.

By the way, Kodakan isn't the only style of music where this happens. Singing monks in 12th and 13th Century Europe sang songs by alternating notes. They called it 'hocket', meaning 'hiccough'. You can also hear a similar thing today in pan pipe playing in some South American music.

Balinese Gamelan musician playing gongs

Do-it-yourself Kodakan

In Kodakan, a tune is split between two players. Each one takes alternate notes. You can try this with an easy tune, such as a nursery rhyme. Try singing this with someone else.

Singer 1	Twin-		twin-		lit-		star,
Singer 2		-kle,		-kle,		-tle	

Singer 1		I		-der		you	
Singer 2	How		won-		what		are.

When you've tried this, try it with another song you know.

You can make it harder by holding on each note until you have to sing the next one.

If you play instruments, try this playing instead of singing.

Track 9: Techno Train, Dave Cooke

When you listen to this track, you really are listening to... the track! Trains are very noisy. The good thing is that most train noises are rhythmic. The wheels on the rails make a rhythm, and old-fashioned steam trains chuff out their steam in rhythm, too. Dave Cooke, who wrote this piece, noticed this and used the rhythms to write 'Techno Train'. Listen to the way the drums and 'sampled' train sounds work together. Dave's family thought it was clever at first, but got a bit fed up in the end. They had to listen to train sounds for days while he found the best ones to 'sample' into his computer.

Techno music

Techno is all about rhythm and pace. Although it sounds complicated, it's based on a really simple idea. You choose a drum rhythm from a drum machine and repeat it loads of times (that's 'looping'). Then you choose some other sounds (real or electronic ones) and record them into a music computer (that's 'sampling'). Now you can change the sounds electronically and loop them round and round as well. The same technique is used in Indie, Garage and Drum 'n' Bass music. There's one main difference between them – how fast they go.

strange, but true

I got rhythm... I got suitcase

The American jazz drummer, Josh Billings, played in the rhythm section of a band called the Blue Blowers. His favourite rhythm instrument was a drum with a difference. He'd made it out of a cardboard suitcase covered in crinkly, brown paper. To get a good, powerful backing rhythm going, he didn't beat the drum, he just gave it lots of hefty kicks.

Suitcases aren't made to be used as drums. Because of the regular kickings they received from Josh, his 'drums' were forever falling to pieces. This meant he was always having to buy new ones. He'd go into a shop, point to a case he fancied and ask to see it. The shop assistant would bring him the case and Josh would begin kicking it – to the absolute horror of everyone in the shop.

Gamelan

A gamelan is a type of percussion orchestra found in many South-East Asian countries. Normally, when you say 'orchestra', it means the instruments and all the musicians. 'Gamelan' just means the instruments. There are at least sixteen different sets of instruments that can be called a gamelan and they vary from country to country. Most of the instruments are made from a special kind of bronze. The makers keep the exact recipe for the metal a closely-guarded secret.

Here are some of the instruments used in a Javanese gamelan, which you can hear on Track 8 'Kodakan'.

The metallophone family is made up of chime bars, vibraphones and glockenspiels. Instruments include the saron and slĕntĕm.

The gong-chime family looks like racks of tuned, old-fashioned, metal kettles. Two types are the bonang and kĕnong.

The gambang is a kind of xylophone with wooden bars.

The gamelan also contains racks of gongs hung on big frames.

Indonesian gamelan orchestra

13

Dance Room

Welcome to the Dance Room. Prance, pogo, or polka into this one because these sounds will really get you moving – not just foot tapping and finger snapping, as in the Rhythm Room, but some serious leaping about.

People have been dancing since Prehistoric times (their feet must be killing them!); on one cave wall in France there's actually a seventeen thousand-year-old painting showing a Stone Age dancer strumming a string bow and wearing funky stag's antlers.

The origin of 'orchestra'

The Ancient Greek word 'orcheomai' (pronounced or-keh-o-ma-ee) — which is where the word orchestra comes from — actually means 'to dance'. Some experts believe that the first music ever played was music to dance to.

Over the centuries, people have danced to celebrate all kinds of things: births, successful harvests, a change of season, a change of luck... just about anything. They've also danced to worship gods, to win prizes, to tell stories and to express feelings of happiness, sadness or anger.

Q. Have you ever tried tap dancing?
A. Yes, but I gave it up. I kept falling in the bath.

Now here's something to think about while you're getting your breath back: a 19th Century music expert called Jean Paul (1763–1825) once said that, 'Music is an invisible dance.' He also said that 'Dancing is silent music!' (although one or two clog dancers would probably disagree with that).

Track 11:
Dance of the Cygnets, Tchaikovsky

Flute

The 'Dance of the Cygnets' is part of composer Tchaikovsky's ballet, 'Swan Lake'. The ballet dancers who pirouetted and pas-de-deuxed to this music danced to tell a story and to express the feelings and ideas of its composer.

'Swan Lake' didn't go down very well at first – probably because the producer of the show had put in some extra bits of music by a different composer! In this piece, see if you can hear oboes and then flutes taking the tune at the beginning.

Pyotr *Ilych Tchaikovsky (1840–1893)*

Pyotr (Peter) Tchaikovsky is the Russian composer who's made millions of people feel happy by writing lots of beautiful music. However, Tchaikovsky himself spent great chunks of his own life feeling miserable and worried.

He was bursting with musical talents. As a little boy, he surprised his parents by listening to tunes on their musical box, then playing them on the piano, just as if he'd written them himself. Rather than going off to study music right away, he first got a job in a law office. He didn't enjoy it much. He finally saw the light and went off to make music and write great things, such as the '1812 Overture' (page 31) and 'The Nutcracker' ballet.

Tchaikovsky also got married, but he didn't enjoy that much either, so he ran away. Not long afterwards, he had a bit of luck. A woman called Madame von Meck said she'd give him lots of money to carry on composing, as long as he kept out of her way and never, ever spoke to her. So he said 'OK!' (by letter, presumably!) and, even when they met at parties a couple of times, they ignored each other completely.

Later in his life, he became really famous and conducted orchestras in places such as America and England. During the last twelve years of his life he spent lots of time living in hotels. Despite all this travelling, he stuck to his daily routine: he got up at 7a.m., had a hot drink, read the Bible for a couple of hours, composed all morning, went for a walk, did more composing, then went to bed (not exactly a 'rock 'n' roll lifestyle', was it?).

In 1893, Tchaikovsky unwisely drank some tap water during the cholera season and died four days later.

Ugly ducklings?

Cygnets are baby swans. It's hard to imagine baby swans dancing — think of their fluffy grey feathers, little webbed feet and stubby wings! Come to think of it, maybe Tchaikovsky got the music right, after all!

Pathetic Symphony

In 1893, Tchaikovsky wrote his sixth symphony, which is often called the 'Pathetic' symphony. That's not because the music is pathetic, but from the French 'pathétique' meaning 'touching', as the music is very moving.

Oboe

Paul Patrick

Paul Patrick, percussion

Most instrumental players specialise in one or two instruments, but percussionists have to know how to play dozens! Some pieces, such as 'Sabre Dance', need several percussion players.

Paul Patrick of the BBC Philharmonic Orchestra says that in some modern pieces he can expect to play at least 25 different instruments!

Track 12:
Sabre Dance, Khachaturian

Khachaturian (pronounced catch-a-TOO-ree-an) was probably inspired to write 'Sabre Dance' by the hair-raising sword dances performed by ferocious Russian Cossack warriors. They leapt around, twirling their sabres and yelling wild cries of defiance.

Khachaturian wrote the 'Sabre Dance' for the full orchestra, but the arrangement on this CD is played by five members of the orchestra's percussion section. You can almost hear those Cossacks rattling their swords!

Listen for the instruments playing the rhythm:

timpani – big, booming tuned drums
side drum – tapping, rattly sound
cymbals – crashing
tambourine – tapping and jingling.

A marimba (see page 48) plays the tune and, at the end, you can just hear a few wavery notes on a vibraphone.

'Sabre Dance' is from a ballet called 'Gayane'.

strange, but true

A percussionist went on tour to Japan with an orchestra as an extra player. He was needed for just one cymbal crash when all the other percussionists were busy and couldn't do it.

Guess what? The extra percussionist lost concentration and missed his cue! He travelled all that way, and cost the orchestra all that money, for nothing!

Aram Ilych Khachaturian (1903-1978)

Young Khachaturian's first brush with music came when he learned the tenor horn and played in his school band. He must have enjoyed it, because he taught himself to play the piano next. He still wasn't satisfied, though. Aram was Armenian and wanted to go to music college in Moscow. The trouble was, he couldn't speak Russian, so he had to learn that first. When he finally went to college, he took up another instrument — the cello. Anyone who could play that many instruments was bound to end up being something like a composer or conductor. He was still only nineteen by this time.

Khachaturian wrote lots of music for ballets and for films. He also wrote the Armenian national anthem — so if you ever see Armenia play football, they'll be singing his tune before the match!

Dippy dance data

Barn dances were first held to celebrate building a new barn. Farmers helped each other and, when they'd finished, all the helpers came round for a party. Nowadays, they don't wait for a new barn, they hold dances regularly in barns (and halls) that are already standing.

In the 1930s, times were tough and money was short in America. To make ends meet, some people held dances in their own homes. Friends and neighbours paid a small entrance fee and everyone danced the night away. These dances were called some odd names: House Stomps, Too Tight Parties and Wang Dang Doodles, for instance. At one 'do', to celebrate the wedding of blues musician, Lightnin' Hopkins, the joint was literally jumpin' – and the walls fell down around their ears.

For one dance performed by the Akan tribe in Ghana, you have to learn forty different body movements to communicate the meaning of the dance properly.

The Italian dance, the Tarantella, is danced to handclapping and rattling tambourines. It's meant to help you get rid of the poison if you're bitten by a tarantula spider – all that twirling and whirling is said to get the poison out of your system.

People have invented all sorts of dances based on animals. One really popular one is the Conga. People form a line, holding each other's hips or shoulders, to make an enormous 'snake', then dance round the room to a rhythmic, Latin-American beat.

At the end of summer, the Hopi Native Americans of Arizona bring hundreds of snakes to their sacred dance ground for a Rain Dance ceremony. They dance with the snakes in their hands and mouths and chant prayers for rain. The Hopi have a great respect for nature and don't harm the snakes.

If you wanted to be hip in the early 20th Century, you did an animal dance. People in Europe and America did new dances called the Grizzly Bear, the Buzzard Lope, the Camel Walk, the Kangaroo Dip and the Bunny Hug.

In the Middle Ages (12th to 15th Centuries) in Europe, there were lots of cases of people affected by an uncontrollable desire to dance in the streets. They weren't happy, it was a dance mania they couldn't control. Outbreaks of this dancing madness happened just after the plague called The Black Death had swept Europe, and people broke out dancing and singing at funerals. Some think it was caused by a chemical in their bread that affected their brain. Others thought it might be a form of mass hysteria (like when the audience screams at a pop band).

strange, but true

The longest Conga ever performed was in the USA, when the Cuban-American people of Miami got together to celebrate living in racial harmony with other locals. One hundred and nineteen thousand, nine hundred and sixty eight people conga'd round the city on 13th March 1988.

Track 13:
Beauty's Theme, Ravel

This music was written by Maurice Ravel (see page 39) as a piano piece for his friend Ida's children, Mimi and Jean. They had to sit next to each other at the piano and use all four of their hands to play it. Later, he arranged the piano piece for orchestra as well and used it for his ballet, called 'Mother Goose'. Each piece in the ballet has a story based on a fairy tale. This one is called 'The Conversation of Beauty and the Beast'. The clarinet plays a warm, gentle tune while Beauty is doing her hair and make-up in front of a mirror. Later, the Beast's tune comes in with a low tune played on contrabassoon (see page 27). 'Beauty's Theme' is calm and romantic. You can just imagine gliding around an enchanted dance hall with your beloved, as you listen.

Flute, clarinet and saxophone

Victoria Bodger, flute, BBC Philharmonic Orchestra

These instruments are all part of the woodwind family. It might seem strange putting them all together, but sometimes one musician can play all three — not at the same time, of course! Here's why.

You get different notes out of each of them by covering or uncovering holes in the tube. They're all much too long to be able to do this with your fingers alone, so they have keys to make it possible. There are hundreds of ways you could arrange the keys but, on these instruments, it's done in a similar way. Once you've learned one, with a bit of extra training, you can play the others. What you do with your mouth to play each one is different, though.

The flute's been around for thousands of years. The modern flute developed from the recorder, although it is made of metal. It is held sideways and you blow across the mouthpiece (see how on page 19). The piccolo is like a very small flute and can reach the highest notes in the modern orchestra.

Jenny Galloway, clarinet, BBC Philharmonic Orchestra

The clarinet sounds different because it is made of wood and you make the sound by blowing down a thin strip of bamboo, called a reed (this is a single reed), attached to the mouthpiece. It vibrates gently as you blow. Modern clarinets were first made in about 1700. Clarinets can play one of the widest ranges of pitch (high and low sounds) in the orchestra.

The saxophone is also made of metal. It was only invented in 1870 – which is recent, as instruments go! Adolphe Saxe, an instrument maker and clarinettist, thought the orchestra needed a new instrument and this is what he invented. It didn't really take off in the orchestra at first, but found a home in jazz and rock music. That was a shame for poor old Saxe, because he died in 1894 before jazz or rock were invented.

Saxophone

strange, but true

Don't stop the dance

The New York police tried to stop one marathon dance (see right) which was being held at the Roseland Ballroom (the biggest dance hall in the world). The organiser called a huge removal van and the dancers danced out of the hall into the van, which then drove to a boat on the river. The dancers danced off the van and onto the boat, which then sailed out to sea – and out of reach of the New York police.

Feets of endurance

During the 1930s, in America, there was a craze for dancing contests. In these, the people who could keep twirling and turning longer than anyone else won prizes. Lots of these 'marathon' dances went on for ages... and ages... and ages.

Mike Ritof and Edith Boudreaux entered a marathon dance contest on 31st August 1930. On New Year's Eve, four months later, they were still dancing (they were allowed 15 minutes' break every hour). They carried on for another three months before finally stopping on April 1st, 1931.

They'd danced for a world-record-breaking total of 5,148 hours, 28 and a half minutes. They got a prize of two thousand dollars.

Marathon dance data

Contestants were often sponsored by businesses. They wore advertisements for the businesses on their clothes. As dancers became too tired to dance, the band increased the tempo (speed) of the music. Why? So they could finish off the last few couples and go home.

In 1932, a man dropped dead at a marathon dance. He'd been dancing for 48 days and nights.

To stop themselves falling asleep contestants would:
a) slap, pinch and kick their partners
b) sniff smelling salts
c) apply packs of ice to various bits of their bodies

One of the most successful marathon dancers ever was Mary 'Hercules' Promitis from Pittsburgh. Mary noticed how professional boxers soaked their hands in vinegar to make them really tough and hard- wearing, so she did the same with her feet... for three weeks! It worked – she ended up with the best pickled bunions in Pittsburgh.

Track 14:
Wedding Dance, Essam Rashad

Belly dancer

From ballet dancing on the last track to belly dancing on this one! 'Wedding Dance' is real celebration music. It's played at Egyptian weddings, for the belly dancers to dance to.

Don't get too dreamy listening to the previous track, or you'll be in for an 'oud' awakening in Wedding Dance. The oud is the name of the instrument which sort of explodes into the room on this track. It's like a guitar with a round body and five pairs of strings (see page 51).

Essam Rashad wrote this tune and plays the oud on it, too. The rhythm is played on Egyptian tabla drums and tambourines.

Do-it-yourself flute

You make a sound on a flute by blowing across a hole, or mouthpiece. Try blowing across the top of an empty plastic bottle. Tuck your lips over your teeth, then try to blow air out down your chin gently. When you can make a good sound, pour a little water into the bottle and try again. The pitch of the sound will change. You could make a line of bottles with different amounts of water in them and blow your own tunes.

19

Track 15: Ceilidh, Steve Everitt

A Ceilidh (say kay-lee) is a Gaelic word meaning, 'a gathering of people.' It's often used in Scotland and Ireland for a musical get-together. At ceilidhs, people make their own entertainment – anyone can bring along instruments and they sing and dance and everyone joins in. These days, ceilidhs may include other things, too.

This tune is a traditional Irish dance tune mixed with modern pop rhythms. Some people call this mixture, 'Riverdance music', after the stage show made popular by Michael Flatley.

Listen for the Irish drum, called a bodhran, at the very start. It's a hollow hand drum, played with a double-ended stick. It contrasts with the drum machine that comes in later on. The tune is played on a whistle and a synthesizer. There are lots of 'twiddly bits' that are hard to play but exciting to listen to and the music gets faster and faster, as it often does in Irish dance tunes. Look out for how the music 'stops' before you expect it to.

Q. How do you know when there's a bodhran player at your door?

A. The knocking gets faster and faster.

Step dancing

Step dancing is the kind of traditional Irish dancing (with modern adaptations) seen in 'Riverdance'. To do it, you have keep the top half of your body still, while your legs and feet perform fast, difficult steps. People used to say that a good Step dancer could dance on eggs without breaking them and carry a pan of water on his head without spilling a drop.

Track 16: Bars of Twelve, Dave Cooke

Dave Cooke wrote this rock'n'roll piece. It's actually 'rock'n'roll' played in 'twelve-bar blues' style (if you want to know what that means, see below). On this track, first you hear just the chords, then each player takes the lead and improvises around the tune. First the saxophone plays, then the electric guitar and, finally, the piano, before they all join together for the end. See if you can guess when each instrument is going to come in.

Do-it-yourself twelve bar blues

'Twelve-bar' means that each section of the music is twelve bars long. Try counting along to the music like this:

1 - 2 - 3 - 4 - 2 - 2 - 3 - 4 - 3 - 2 - 3 - 4

4 - 2 - 3 - 4 - 5 - 2 - 3 - 4 →

and so on, until you begin a bar with 12. You should find that, when you get there, the music is ready to 'go round again'. Usually, there are only three chords, used in the same pattern again and again.

Each player improvises (see page 11) to the twelve-bar pattern.

Dance around the world

In almost every part of the world people have made up dances to fit their own traditional music. Dance can be 'folk' dancing, classical dancing (formally taught and sometimes part of religious ceremonies) or just social (at family or community get-togethers). Here are just a few types of dance from around the world that are on the Blue Peter CD.

Track 15
'Ceilidh', Steve Everitt
Irish folk dancing has been made popular in recent years by mixing it with pop music. In the modern dances, many traditional steps are kept, but steps from other types of folk dancing (such as Flamenco from Spain) have been added. Some of the dancers wear heavy shoes and the clicking they make is part of the rhythm of the dance.

Track 16
'Bars of Twelve', Dave Cook
Rock 'n' roll music came about in the 1950s in America. It developed from the rhythms brought over by slaves from Africa, mixed with American Country and Western and 'blues' music. Elvis Presley was one of the people who made it famous. Rock 'n' roll dances are very energetic and are danced by couples, who rock 'n' roll to the beat.

Track 18
'Turkey in the Straw', Traditional
This tune is a barn dance-type tune. In barn dancing, the whole family joins in the simple dances. There's a 'caller', who shouts out the moves so they all know what to do next.

Track 14
'Wedding Dance', Essam Rashad
Belly dancing is traditional at Egyptian weddings. As the name suggests, the dancers dance not only with their hands and feet, but wobble their tummy and hips around in time to the music. Try it sometime – they say it keeps you very fit and isn't as easy as it looks to do it properly!

Track 49
'Funky Dhol', Kuljit Bhamra
This music is known as Bhangra. It comes from a harvest celebration dance from Northern India. It's a classical dance with set moves representing the reapers cutting the corn with a scythe. More recently this has been brought up-to-date as the music has been mixed with Western pop music, but many of the traditional moves are still used.

Track 40
'Denka', Traditional
Singing and dancing are part of everyday life in Africa. This rhythmic dance tune is played in West Africa to celebrate the birth of a baby.

Track 3
'Mambo', Leonard Bernstein
This piece of music comes from Bernstein's musical, but a Mambo is a dance invented in the 1940s in Cuba. Like so many Latin American dances, it mixes African rhythms with Spanish rhythms – a very exciting mix that makes you want to get up and move.

Track 35
'Air on a G String', Bach
From the 16th to the end of the 18th Centuries, every royal court in Western Europe (particularly France, Germany, Austria and Italy) had its resident composers and musicians. They wrote pieces for special occasions, ceremonies and for dancing. A suite was a series of dances. Some of the dances were the pavan, galliard, salterello and gigue.

Track 7
'Straight No Chaser', Thelonious Monk
Jazz music started in New Orleans in America. It's a mixture of Spanish, French and African music. Jazz dance became a cool thing to do in the 1920s and it became popular again in the late 1990s, with Swing (Jazz) Bands all over the place and lots of young Americans wanting to learn Swing Dance like their great grandparents!

Track 12
'Sabre Dance', Khatchaturian
Russian Cossack Dancers are famous for amazing athletic dancing. The male dancers squat on their heels and throw their legs out sideways very fast, so it looks as if they're bouncing with their feet off the ground. The Cossacks were fierce warriors and you can imagine them flashing their swords dangerously as they dance.

Track 11
'Dance of the Cygnets' Tchaikovsky
Ballet is the art of stories in dance. It was invented in the courts of Italy and France in the 16th and 17th Centuries. You have to be fitter to do ballet than for most sports. Footballers have been given ballet exercises to strengthen their muscles! Ballet is based on formal movements, which have to be practised over and over again to train the muscles.

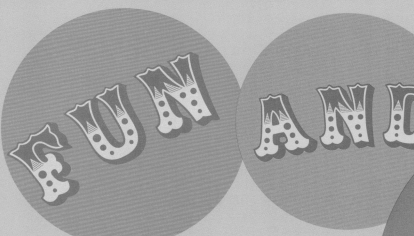

FUN AND

Q. What do you call a banjo maker?
A. A banjineer.

GAMES Room

This is the room where the musicians and composers put on their silly hats and have a bit of fun. As you'll hear, the music is great for brightening a dull day or lightening a murky mood. This room has a carnival atmosphere, as if the composers were taking a break from being serious and playing around with their music.

A music writer once described how some of the Dave Brubeck Quartet's music (see page 29) was played to soldiers in a hospital. The soldiers had been through a really bad time and were feeling miserable. They had spent months hardly moving or speaking. When the music was played to them the effect was astonishing. Within minutes they perked up and began moving their bodies and tapping their feet in time to the music, and they all looked happier than they'd done in ages. Now that really is instant musical medicine! One of the tunes made famous by Dave Brubeck's quartet is on Track 23.

Banjo

Q. You can tune a banjo, but how do you 'tuna' fish?

A. By adjusting its scales!

Track 18: Turkey in the Straw, Traditional

No one's really sure who first dreamed up this traditional American tune, and the turkey in the title was probably turned into a roast dinner at least two hundred years ago. It's the sort of tune that the American country folk, called hillbillies, would have jigged around to when they had musical get-togethers.

Time to get your checked shirts and cowboy boots on, folks!

Accordion

Funky Chickens

'Colonel' Tom Parker was the manager of the famous rock 'n' roller, Elvis Presley. The Colonel thought 'Turkey In the Straw' was great for dancing, too. Before he was Elvis's boss, he ran a fairground sideshow. He charged people to come and watch an amazing 'chicken-disco', where his performing poultry shimmied and strutted to 'Turkey in the Straw'. Cruel Colonel Parker hadn't actually trained his bantams to boogie! He just covered a sheet of hot metal with straw, then shoved the chickens on top. They had no choice but to leap about to save their soles (or whatever it is hens have on the bottom of their feet) from burning.

Acoustic guitar

Bluegrass music

Bluegrass music is a branch of American country music which started in the 1940s in Kentucky. Kentucky is called the Blue Grass State. They say the grass there is so lush it looks almost blue instead of green.

Instruments found in Bluegrass music are the fiddle, banjo, guitar and mandolin. A plucked double bass accompanies them and there's sometimes a drum kit. Occasionally, you can also hear an accordion or piano, too.

The first real Bluegrass band was Bill Monroe and his Blue Grass Boys (Bill played the mandolin). They based their music on very old American songs and tunes, then added the kind of beat you can hear on the 'Turkey in the Straw' track.

Track 19:
Trumpet Concerto, Hummel

You can tell that the soloist on this track is enjoying himself. He's been given the star part in Hummel's bright and brassy 'Trumpet Concerto', which is *tootally* delightful!

This is an example of how to play an instrument very quickly and accurately. To get all those notes to happen in the right places, the trumpeter has to 'tongue' the mouthpiece of the trumpet. To do this, the soloist on this track, Martin Winter (see page opposite), blows into his trumpet but 'says' these 'words' with his tongue:

daga DA daga DA daga DA daga daga-daga DA DA daga-daga DA

The capital DAs last longer than the others. Listen carefully and see if you can hear where he does this in the fast bits.

Q **Why are trumpets like pirates?**

A **Because they're murder on the high Cs!**

French horn

JOHANN HUMMEL (1778-1837)

Johann Hummel was taught by Mozart, and he was a brilliant pianist. When he was nine years old he went all round Europe on a concert tour. He wrote mostly piano music, but found time to write other pieces as well, like the 'Trumpet Concerto' in this Room.

Trombone

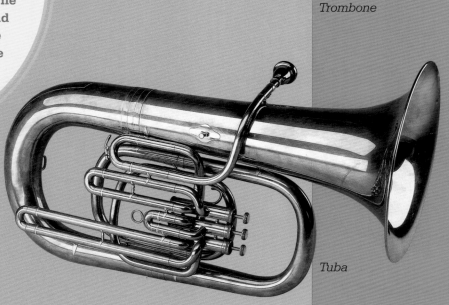

Tuba

Brass instruments

Trumpets were first made from people blowing into conch shells to signal to each other. Today they are made of brass.

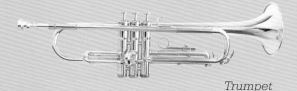

Trumpet

Modern trumpets have three valves to make it easier to play all the notes. See the story of the birth of the modern trumpet on the right.

The French horn is another brass instrument. It developed around the 1650s in France. It came from the crescent-shaped hunting horns used at the time. It is played by putting one hand inside the big bell of the instrument to alter the tone.

The trombone is a nine-foot (that's about 2.66m) brass tube folded in the middle. Its ancestor was a medieval instrument called the sackbut or sagbutt, which means 'push pull'. It has a sliding metal tube to alter the pitch. It was once used in a lot of church music but now plays everything from jazz to military band and orchestral music.

The tuba is the newest addition to the brass family. It was invented in 1835 by a Prussian bandmaster and his builder friend who wanted to make a deep brass instrument for their band. It had a much better tone than older bass brass instruments, such as the serpent and the ophicleide. The lowest modern 'tuba' is the sousaphone, which is so big it winds around the player like a giant brass snake.

Q. What do you call a baby tuba?
A. A one-ba!

Q How do you clean a sousaphone?
A With a tuba toothpaste.

Birth of the trumpet

Bugles were horns used to send signals during battles. You could only get five or six notes out of them. The story goes that one day a bugle boy was playing and a bullet went straight through the tube. He noticed that the pitch changed and that he could play different notes. This gave people the idea of putting other holes in brass instruments. At first they tried covering and uncovering the holes with keys, like on a woodwind instrument, but it didn't work that well. In the 1800s, Heinrich Stölzel and Friedrich Blühmel worked out a way to make more notes using valves. The valves allowed the air to travel down a different length of tube and change the note. The modern trumpet was born.

Louis Armstrong, a famous jazz trumpeter

MARTIN WINTER, TRUMPET

Martin Winter, of the BBC Philharmonic Orchestra, plays the trumpet solo in this recording of Hummel's 'Trumpet Concerto'. When you're sitting in the orchestra, you have to play just the way the conductor wants. When you're a soloist, you can play your part more expressively.

Martin says it's pretty lonely playing on your own. You can put a bit of your own personality into the music, but everyone can hear exactly what you're playing (and if you play a wrong note).

CAMILLE SAINT-SAËNS (1835-1921)

'I live in music as a fish lives in water,' said Camille (although he would have said it in French, of course). Another one of his sayings was, 'I produce music as an apple tree produces apples.'

Young Camille was interested in astronomy and archaeology. He was a real star at digging up good tunes (groan!), and started composing when he was only three years old!

Track 20: Elephant, Saint-Saëns

This track features an animal which does a fair bit of trumpeting itself. Camille Saint-Saëns wrote 'Elephant' (plus a whole zoo's-worth of other animal tunes) as part of his 'Carnival of the Animals', as a bit of fun to entertain his adult friends during a holiday.

The tune is played on a double bass. People usually think of instruments that make a deep noise, like the double bass, as playing slow music. Big, heavy animals are usually slow too, so that's why Saint-Saëns wrote the music like this. When you listen to how the bass is played on this track, you realise that big can be beautiful too.

Saint-Saëns wanted to be thought of as a 'serious' composer so, after the holiday, he banned all public performances of his 'Carnival of the Animals' until after he died. It had its first public performance just after his death in 1922.

Do-it-yourself double bass

Take a heavy cardboard box and place it with the open side on the floor (open out the flaps flat, if you can). Then you need a broom and a piece of thick string about 1.5m long. Make a hole in the bottom of the box, big enough to push the broom handle through. Push the broom through from underneath. Make another, small hole and thread the string up through it. Tie a big knot in the end of the string that's inside the box. Stand on one of the open flaps of the box, pull the string up and tie it to the top of the broom handle. stretching it as tight as you can. Pluck your one-string bass with the other hand. Experiment with tightening and loosening the string.

Track 21: The Sorcerer's Apprentice, Dukas

You might have seen the Walt Disney film 'Fantasia' (the original one, or the 2000 version). In the movie, Mickey Mouse plays the Sorcerer's Apprentice. The idea is that a learner magician decides to have a bit of magical fun while the boss is away, but gets out of his depth. Just imagine all the things you find in any old sorcerer's house (you know, pots, pans, toes of frog, eyes of newt... that sort of thing – but no CDs, computer screens or personal stereos!) dancing about on their own. Anyway, the boss comes home just in time to put things right before there's too much damage! You can read about the composer of this piece, Paul Dukas, on page 47.

Double reeds

Oboes (as on Track 11), bassoons and the cor anglais are all wind instruments that use double reeds. See how this works by taking a drinking straw. Flatten one end and cut the corners off, as shown. Put 2–3cm of the cut end between your lips, hold hard and blow. You should be able to make a 'reedy' sound, with practice.

The oboe and bassoon

These are woodwind instruments, too (see page 18). Take the sound you made with a straw, above, shove it down a 2m wooden tube and you've got a bassoon.

Of course, it's not quite that simple. You need your reed, then you have to bend the tube in two, so you can manage to hold it. You need to put finger holes in the right place to get different notes. You also need to put keys and springs on the outside so you can reach the holes. Then you just need to learn to play it!

The oboe works in the same way, using a double reed.

Oboe

The oboe sounds very 'nasal'. Try pinching your nose hard, then sing a tune, to get some idea. Oboists have to learn circular breathing, like didgeridoo players (see page 9).

Both the oboe and bassoon come in jumbo-sized versions, too. There's a bigger version of the oboe called the cor anglais, or English horn. It's bigger than an oboe, with a hooked metal tube sticking out of the top. The biggest bassoon, the contrabassoon, is one of the lowest-sounding instruments in the orchestra.

DAVID CHATWIN, BASSOON

David Chatwin of the BBC Philharmonic took to the bassoon because it's so big! The bassoon is often called the 'clown' in the orchestra because it's good at playing bouncy tunes like the theme from 'The Sorcerer's Apprentice'. It's very difficult to play well and you need to practise a lot to jump around like the three bassoons in the version of Take Five (Track 21) on the CD. If you listen carefully, you can hear the keys clattering.

Track 22: Cats' Duet, Rossini

This song is by an Italian composer called Rossini. Its proper name in Italian is 'Duetto Buffo di Due Gatti'. Rossini wrote the words himself: 'Meow, meow...' (Sorry, in Italian, that's...'Miau, miau...'). You probably don't think that took much doing, and you'd be right. But the thing about Rossini was that he could turn any old rubbish into great music. Turning cats meowing into music wasn't much of a challenge to a genius like him.

The song is meant to be performed by two sopranos, but on this recording, all the singing and the extra cat noises are performed by only one. It's really hard to do, and even the most famous opera singers never quite get it right (in fact, some of them just simply refuse to do it).

GIOACCHINO ROSSINI (1792-1868)

Rossini was quite lazy and hated getting up in the mornings. He often composed in bed. Once, he'd written an aria for one of his operas and dropped it under the bed. Anyone else would have got out of bed and picked it up. Not Rossini! He got a fresh piece of paper and wrote a new one.

But Rossini could work very hard under pressure. He composed the whole of his opera 'The Barber of Seville' in just three weeks. To be honest, Gioacchino did cheat a bit. He actually recycled the overture from another opera that had flopped a few years back for 'The Barber of Seville'.

This all happened in Naples in 1816. Unfortunately, he'd forgotten that someone else had written a popular version of 'The Barber of Seville' a few years before. His name was Paisiello, and he <u>hadn't</u> forgotten. On the opening night he sent some friends round to wreck the show. They shouted and hissed all the way through. The singers got rattled and made all kinds of mistakes... then someone let a cat loose on the stage. It was a disaster! After that night, though, things went better. They took the show to London and New York. Rossini and his 'Barber of Seville' are still really famous. Paisiello and his... aren't!

strange, but true

Happy birthday, dear doggie

Rossini was a bit weird. He wrote tunes for dogs too. Every year he'd write his pet pooch some birthday music as a special present. Aaah!

Q. Why did the oboist have two books in her hand?

A. Because she needed a 'double read' to play.

Track 23:
Take Five, Paul Desmond

Paul Desmond (see right) wrote his 'Take Five' hit in 1959 and named it after the unusual number of beats in the bar in this tune (see Counting past four, below) – not after the length of their tea breaks, as some people thought. This number was the first 'million-seller' jazz single ever. It gave lots of pop fans their first taste of the massive musical feast that is jazz. Many of them remained hooked on jazz for the rest of their lives.

'Take Five' made absolutely tons of money and, being the completely nice person he was, Paul donated his royalties (the part of the money he got every time a record was sold) to the Red Cross.

PAUL DESMOND (1924-1977)

Paul Desmond was a jazz composer, alto saxophonist, and a right laugh. His real name was Breitenfeld but he didn't fancy that as a jazz musician's name. So he looked in the telephone directory, saw the name Desmond, and thought he'd have that name instead.

In 1951 he formed the Dave Brubeck Quartet with the jazz pianist, Dave Brubeck. They were soon jetting around the world, doing a mind-boggling three hundred concerts a year (along with two other musicians, of course).

In 1956, a new drummer, called Joe Morello, joined the Quartet. Paul wasn't keen on the marathon drum solos that Joe liked belting out. While the new boy played, Paul went backstage and read his book. Paul was so put out by Joe's drum bashing that he wouldn't speak to him for him a whole year, but after that they became the best of mates.

strange, but true

How many are there in your Quartet?

When the Dave Brubeck Quartet split up in 1967, Paul Desmond said he was going to write a book about their adventures. He claimed he would call it, How many are there in your Quartet? (that's what people were forever asking him and the band – think about it, it's not a very bright question). He never wrote the book, though. He said the only place he could write was on the beach and that the sand kept getting in his typewriter.

Counting past four

At the start of a song, bands often count 'one, two, three, four.' That's so they can all start together. Sometimes, you have to count further than that. 'Take Five' has five beats in the bar instead of the more usual four, so you have to count to five.

The Dave Brubeck Quartet, (see above), used to go in for other weird numbers of beats in the bar, too. In 'Unsquare Dance' there are seven beats in a bar, and in 'Blue Rondo à la Turk', there are nine.

In a lot of modern classical music you can hear unusual numbers of beats in a bar. In 'Mars' from 'The Planets', composer Gustav Holst wanted a marching rhythm, but he wanted it to come out sounding all wrong. So he put an extra beat in each bar. Try marching to that!

Igor Stravinsky (1882–1971) loved to play with unusual numbers of beats in the bar. One of his most famous experiments is 'Dance of the Adolescents' from his ballet, 'The Rite of Spring'. The number of beats changes so often, it gives a very exciting feeling of 'moving on'.

The Crash! Bang! Room

Right, now it's time for dread...doom... and drums! Ever since the first prehistoric look-out beat a hollow bit of wood with a stick to warn his mates that the enemy was on the way, drums and percussion instruments have often been linked with feelings of fear, alarm and excitement.

Don't worry, though, this room's not all boom, doom and gloom. There are some celebrations too, such as the '1812 Overture' (Track 25)... listen out for that extra-spectacular big bang at the end.

Other pieces in this room suggest noisy things, such as monsters banging and crashing around, or warriors preparing for battle. Then the final piece, Joseph Schwantner's seriously scary 'Percussion Concerto', just has to be the perfect backing track for a haunted house movie. Talk about things that go bump in the night (...not to mention, crash...bang...wallop!).

strange, but true

Crash! Bang! Silence...

A cymbal player at a performance of Tchaikovsky's 'Romeo and Juliet Overture' was supposed to make a sound like swords clashing in the part where the sweethearts' two families are scrapping. He was supposed to do this by briskly brushing the cymbals against each other.

He didn't quite get it right and sort of crashed his cymbals directly onto each other.

The next thing he knew, the cymbals were sealed together because he'd forced all the air from between them and created a vacuum. Try as he might, he couldn't get them apart. After a while, the audience noticed him struggling and all began laughing. Then the rest of the orchestra noticed and they all burst out laughing too!

Track 25:
1812 Overture, Tchaikovsky

Tchaikovsky didn't really want to write the '1812 Overture', but he needed the money. The people who organised the 1880 Moscow Exhibition wanted a piece to be played outside in the square. Napoleon Bonaparte had tried to capture the city 68 years before, but was forced to retreat because the winter weather was so bad. Somehow, they'd only just got around to celebrating this, and wanted something noisy because it was a big square.

Tchaikovsky decided to use everything they'd got — a massive orchestra, a military band, the bells of the cathedral and all the cannons they could find. To keep everyone happy, he worked in the Russian national anthem and the French national anthem, 'La Marseillaise', too.

Track 26: Haichijo, Traditional

This is a piece of traditional music from Japan. There's an island off the southern coast of Japan called 'Hachijo Jima'. That could be where the name of the piece comes from. The music is played on a shakuhachi (bamboo flute) and taiko (drums). The musicians manage to make it really exciting to listen to by suddenly going quiet, then building up to full volume again.

Japanese music

Music is used for all kinds of occasions in Japan. The main religions in Japan are Buddhism and Shintoism. They use music to accompany their ceremonies.

There are also lots of different kinds of Japanese drama and entertainment that all need music. There's Kabuki, traditional Japanese theatre, and Bumraku, which uses puppets. In another traditional theatre form, called Noh, there's no speaking at all and the music helps to tell you what the actors are feeling. Then there's Gagaku, which is music used as a background to all sorts of happenings in the Imperial Court.

There's a huge number of Japanese instruments, but here are some of the commonest ones:

The taiko is the drum that you can hear on Haichijo.

The shakuhachi is a bamboo flute, also on Track 26.

There are also lots of Japanese stringed instruments:

The shamisen is a kind of lute with just three strings.

The koto is amazing. It has up to seventeen strings that you pluck. The player can change the tuning of the strings because the frets can be moved.

Many electronic keyboards are made in Japan. If you can get a look at one, see what sounds it can make. You may find some of the instruments mentioned here.

Japanese koto player

Musician playing shakuhachi

Taiko drummer

Track 27:
Crosstimes, Dave Cooke

Dave Cooke's stirring 'Crosstimes' has the same feel of excitement about it as the last track, but it's not half as warlike. There's more of an atmosphere of 'going places', as the various instruments seem to chatter excitably about their trip.

'Crosstimes' was specially written for this CD. It got its title from the two rhythms that make up the piece. There's a main tune pattern built around six beats, and a drum rhythm that's based on four beats, but these take the same amount of time to play. This gives it a very exciting feel as the patterns work against each other.

You can have a go at using different beats together yourself, if you have someone to try it with. (see Do-it-yourself Crosstimes, below).

Do-it-yourself Crosstimes

You need two people for this. Each pick a line from the diagram below: the top line counts six in the same time that the bottom line counts four. Count along your lines together. Notice how some of the numbers come together and some are 'in between' each other.

If you get it right, the rhythm should sound a bit like someone saying 'Loadsa money, loadsa money, loadsa money...' You can actually do this on your own, but it's even trickier. Tap on a table top or on your knees. Use your right hand for one rhythm and your left for the other.

Track 28:
Throstle's Nest Junction,
Sir Peter Maxwell Davies

Even the normal instruments on this track are played in strange ways. You have to rub a bass drum with your wet fingers, rub a tam-tam (a big gong) with a plastic soap dish and use a double bass bow to play a cymbal.

Sir Peter Maxwell Davies wrote this piece especially for the BBC Philharmonic Orchestra. Throstle's Nest Junction was part of a railway line in Salford where Sir Peter lived when he was a boy. This part of the railway was below street level. There was a huge hole to let out the steam, and rumbling and groaning noises came out of it whenever a train went over the junction. He vividly recalls hearing the train wheels screeching. When he wrote 'Throstle's Nest Junction', he put some of these sounds into his score.

The music certainly sounds like the crashing, rattling and screeching of monstrous steam trains – and they sound pretty scary, especially if you were a small boy. Listen to this track and see what you think.

Q Did you hear about the band director who got zapped by lightning?
A Yeah! He must've been a good conductor!

Sir Peter Maxwell Davies

Sir Peter Maxwell Davies (known as 'Max' to all his friends in the music world) comes from Salford and studied music in Manchester.

He has travelled all over the world, but lives and composes in the Orkney Islands, off northern Scotland.

Even though he's a famous composer, Max had a bit of bother in America. He went with the BBC Philharmonic Orchestra to Las Vegas as part of a big US tour. People were trying to ring him while he was there. Everybody thought he was staying at the Flamingo Hotel, but they couldn't seem to get hold of him whenever they called.

He <u>was</u> there, but somehow the hotel's computer had turned him from 'Maxwell Davies' into 'Mavis' so it couldn't find him when people rang.

The composer thought this was so funny that he invented a character called Mavis and wrote a piece called 'Mavis in Las Vegas', about her visiting some of the places he'd seen.

Brain teaser

Q What job involves doing all these things?:
● Dragging heavy chains over a big sheet of metal
● Shaking a biscuit tin full of things that rattle
● Scraping a plate with a knife
● Popping balloons with a pin
● Scraping a blackboard with your fingernails

A Being a percussionist in Throstle's Nest Junction!

In the Hall of the Mountain King, Grieg

This is a piece from 'Peer Gynt', by Edvard Grieg, and there are definitely monsters on this track. They're the ugly, underground sort known as trolls. Listen to how the tension builds up. Grieg tiptoes us into the Hall Of the Mountain King, using just the low instruments of the orchestra — plucked cellos and double basses, and bassoons. But the trolls still manage to hear us... the tune works its way higher and higher up the orchestra until everyone is playing.

It gets louder and louder as more instruments join in. The music gets faster and the tension mounts, until it's as if we're running out of the caves and down the mountainside to safety. There are lots of crashes and bangs at the end. Also listen to how the whole orchestra stops and starts exactly together in the last few bars (see 'Tight playing' below). The bottom sounds hold the sound of a big orchestra together. In this piece they have their moment of glory and sound dark and mysterious.

A boy walked into a room and saw Grieg playing 'In the Hall of the Mountain King' backwards.
Boy: But I thought you were dead!
And why are you playing backwards?
Grieg: I am dead. I'm just decomposing.

Tight playing

When musicians play together, they sometimes have slightly different ideas about how the rhythm goes. When that happens, notes that you should hear at the same time are not quite together. This makes the music feel a bit 'mushy' or 'loose'.

When the rhythm is absolutely together, musicians say, 'That was really tight!' You can hear some really tight playing at the end of 'In the Hall of the Mountain King'. The whole orchestra sounds like one person playing.

Rock and jazz bands often put a big, long chord at the end of a piece where they improvise with the notes a lot. They enjoy the 'messing around' but they always like a 'tight' ending.

Edvard Grieg (1843-1907)

When he was a child, the Norwegian composer, Edvard Grieg, wanted to be a vicar, but his piano-playing mum insisted on giving him music lessons. Not long after, Ole Bull (the famous Norwegian violinist) heard him play and told his mum to send him to a famous music school in Germany.

After that, there was no stopping Edvard. By the time he was in his mid-twenties, he'd composed the 'Peer Gynt Suite', written his famous 'Piano Concerto in A minor' and opened a music school. By the time he was twenty-nine, the government of Norway was so impressed with what he'd done for Norwegian music that they decided to give him his old age pension forty years early as a way of saying, 'Thanks, keep up the good work!'

Strange, but true

Haven't I heard that somewhere before?

Edvard Grieg was once out in a boat fishing with a composer friend. All of a sudden, he got an idea for a great new tune. He took a bit of paper out of his pocket and scribbled the tune down. He put the paper down and went back to his fishing. A few seconds later, a gust of wind blew the paper into the water. Edvard didn't notice, but his friend did. The friend rescued the note, took a quick look at it, then pocketed it, without saying anything.

Not long afterwards, the friend began whistling the tune that he'd seen on the paper. Edvard was amazed and asked his friend what it was. His friend told him it was an idea he'd just had. Edvard was dumbstruck. He thought they'd both had exactly the same idea at the same time.

Timbale

Track 30:
Percussion Concerto, Joseph Schwantner

In a concerto, the music is played by the orchestra with a 'star player', called the soloist. Concertos have been written for just about every instrument you can imagine: piano, violin, clarinet, and so on. The soloist usually stands or sits at the front of the orchestra to play. In this piece, the soloist is playing percussion. The percussion section in the orchestra is normally at the back, so it's quite unusual to have drums and other percussion instruments at the front for this piece.

In the part of the concerto on this CD, the soloist plays a tune on drums. Tunes normally have a lot of different notes in them. Individual drums don't make many notes, so you need a lot of different drums to play a tune, and they take up a lot of room.

Listen out for the bright, tinkling sound of the crotales. These look like a row of tiny cymbals attached to a board. In the last part, the soloist plays a very complicated tune on the marimba (read about marimbas on page 48).

Do-it-yourself percussion

You can make yourself a percussion section using lots of kitchen things (but do ask permission first). Tap upside-down plates, bowls, mugs and jugs with metal spoons. Or tap the bottoms of saucepans and colanders with a wooden spoon. Strike a cheese-grater with a chopstick, or ching two saucepan lids together. Do it all gently – kitchen things aren't made to be hit hard.

JOSEPH SCHWANTNER

Joseph Schwantner was born in Chicago. He is Professor of Composition at the Eastman School of Music in New York, and his music has won many prizes, including the Pulitzer Prize.

Joseph was always interested in music and began to learn classical guitar when he was eight. He got into trouble with his music teacher because he began 'improving' the pieces he was learning. Eventually the teacher realised she wasn't going to stop him doing this and suggested he wrote some music of his own to bring to the lesson.

Big Bangs

Brain teaser

How do you make a gong or cymbal change its pitch after you've hit it?

Answer: Lower it slowly into a big tub of water. It sounds like a tape slowing down. Joseph Schwantner uses this sound in another part of his 'Percussion Concerto'.

Composers have used all kinds of ways to make big bangs in their music, usually with percussion. Apart from the cannons Tchaikovsky used in the '1812 Overture', here are some of the noisy objects that have popped up in music over the years:

Giuseppe Verdi used anvils (the big lump of metal on which a blacksmith hammers and shapes the things he makes) because a scene in his opera 'Il Trovatore' ('The Troubador') was set in… a blacksmith's workshop.

Gustav Mahler wrote for a 'hammer' (a big lump of wood like a tea chest, hit with another big lump of wood) in his 'Sixth Symphony'. This sounds like a very big judge's gavel (the small wooden hammer a judge uses to get 'Silence in Court!'), sealing your fate for ever (yikes)!

Richard Strauss used thunder sheets (huge sheets of metal hanging on a frame), to represent thunder in the mountains in 'Alpine Symphony'.

strange, but true

Silence is golden

Just to soothe you after all that racket, John Cage wrote a piece in 1952 that consists of four minutes and thirty-three seconds of silence. This is supposed to be played on the piano, but has been arranged for other instruments… no, really!

Hans Werner Henze wrote a piece called 'The Tedious Way to Natascha Ungeheuer's Place' in which Japanese percussionist, Stomu Yamash'ta, had to play a wrecked car.

The biggest bass drum in the world was used in the Royal Festival Hall in London. It measured four metres across and made a huge bang.

Room of Dreams

Music has the power to make people dream and take them to all sorts of wonderful places. This tuneful travelling all takes place in your head and you don't even have to fall asleep to do it. Hearing certain sounds seems to pull a musical trigger that we've all got in our brain. You might be passing a busker in the street, or relaxing to a new CD, when you suddenly hear something special or familiar (just a few notes will do it). Before you know it, all kinds of pictures, feelings and memories flood into your mind. Hearing an old song can start you dreaming about the past. Or music from another part of the world (like track 36?) can remind you of a special holiday.

Keyboards

'The Gift of Life' was played on a Yamaha grand piano. The piano as we know it was 'invented' in the early 1800s, but keyboards have been around a lot longer than that. Harpsichords, clavichords, virginals and spinets were around from 1500 and looked a bit like pianos.

In a piano, the strings are played with little, felt-covered hammers. In a harpsichord, the strings are gently plucked with quills and sound rather like playing a guitar with hundreds of fingernails.

The keyboard is still an exciting instrument that keeps changing. They can be so small that you can carry them under your arm, or very big indeed.

Grand piano

Track 32:
The Gift of Life, Dave Cooke

The piano really seems to 'talk' to you on this track. The music is simply beautiful and beautifully simple. It's played in a thoughtful way, as if the pianist's thinking of something enjoyable in the past.

The piano repeats the first musical 'phrase' (the introduction) a few times. Then the strings join in. After that, the piano pours its heart out for a few seconds before going back to that first tune.

So what's the music 'saying'? Well, it will say different things to each person. Use your imagination and it may inspire you. Music's been known to inspire works of art, such as poetry, plays or paintings.

Track 33: Sunrise, Ravel

This is from a ballet called 'Daphnis and Chloë'. A famous dance arranger called Diaghilev asked Ravel to write this ballet for him. He wanted the well-known dancer, Nijinsky, to perform in it. Ravel started writing 'Daphnis and Chloë' in 1909, but didn't finish it for another three years. He was a very slow and careful worker. He once said that it could take him years to write just a single note.

The ballet tells the story of a young Sicilian shepherd called Daphnis. He falls in love with a beautiful 'nymph' girl called Chloë. Just when he thinks things are going well, pirates kidnap her and it seems she's in real danger. In the nick of time, a god called Pan turns up and saves her.

Lots of people think 'Daphnis and Chloë' is Ravel's great masterpiece. It was a huge success when it was first performed. As well as the beautiful, romantic music, there was Nijinsky's dancing and gorgeous stage scenery, created by an artist called Leon Bakst.

The whole piece is a sort of sound picture. Listen to the part that's on the CD and imagine the scene. It's dawn in the countryside. There are rustlings and twitterings as birds and worms and ants wake up. Chloë is in her grotto (a sort of cave – only a nice one). Daphnis is driving his sheep across the meadow. They are about to meet. And then, as the sun finally peeps above the horizon, they see each other for the first time. It's love at first sight!

Ravel's Bolero

Probably Ravel's most famous piece of music is his 'Bolero'. It starts very quietly, then more and more instruments join in and it gets louder and louder (called a crescendo), until they're making a fantastic noise. Ravel said he was inspired to write it by heavy industry. He also said that 'Bolero' was his only masterpiece, adding, 'Unfortunately, there's no music in it!'

Maurice Ravel (1875-1937)

When the French composer, Maurice Ravel, was a child, he had piano lessons. He didn't like them one bit. His mother had to bribe him to do each hour's practice.

As he grew up, he got into all sorts of music. He liked jazz and gypsy fiddling and gamelan music (as on Track 8), which he first heard at the World Exhibition in 1889. In those days, there were no CDs, radios or jet aeroplanes, so most people rarely heard music from around the world.

When World War I broke out in 1914, Maurice was desperate to be a soldier, but he was too small, so he became an ambulance driver instead. Being in the war didn't suit him at all and he came back badly shaken. Not long after this, his mum died, which shook him even more. Still, he carried on composing until he got a terrible brain disease during the 1930s. He decided to have it treated, but the operation went wrong and he died.

Simon Butterworth, who plays bass clarinet and saxophone for the BBC Philharmonic Orchestra, says he once held one note a beat too long in Ravel's 'Bolero' and got out of step with the orchestra. He tried to get back into time, but got in such a mess that by the end of the piece the orchestra had several bars left to play when he had already finished! Everyone knows 'Bolero' well, so he couldn't pretend nothing was wrong – he worries whenever he has to play it, now.

Simon Butterworth

Track 34:
Lullaby, Traditional

Native American music is based around the voice, sometimes with drum accompaniment. This beautiful lullaby, sung by some ladies from the Lumbee nation, has very simple words. They mean 'As you think, so it shall be, or, 'What you think, you create.' It reflects the way they feel about their relationship with the world.

Lots of old Native American religions said that all the natural world (animals, plants, and even the weather) was cleverer and more powerful than humans. So they thought it was a good idea to take notice of these things. They had dreams which brought them messages and words of wisdom from nature. Then they sang and danced about what they'd learned. This was their way of telling the rest of the tribe about the dream and thanking the spirits for the dream.

Lumbee women singing

Native American music

The most important instruments the Native Americans use are their voices. They sometimes use some rhythmic rattling and drumming, or flutes and pipes, too. Most Native Americans had a nomadic way of life, following the bison herds, which provided everything they needed for everyday life. This lifestyle meant that they couldn't carry heavy instruments around.

Almost all Native American tribes have a singing tradition. Their music varies according to where they live. The ones who live out on the prairies sing in powerful, high-pitched voices that carry across wide open spaces. Others, who live in villages, sing in deeper, bass voices.

Track 35:
Air on a G String, Bach

Almost everyone who hears the 'Air on a G String' says they find it relaxing and soothing. Lots of people know the tune really well because it was used as the background music in a famous cigar advertisement on TV some years ago.

The 'Air' is a part of one of Bach's musical suites. 'Suite' is the name for a piece of music that is made up of a chain of linked pieces for dancing to. If you listen to the other bits of the suite (it's Number 3), you'll find that they're quite lively, not like this relaxing tune.

An 'air' is a nice, simple tune written for singing or performing on a solo instrument. This one got its name when a musician arranged it for violin and piano in the 19th Century. He decided that the tune should just be played on the lowest and richest-sounding string of the violin: the G string.

 The musician's wife came back home and found this note:

Gone Chopin, have Liszt, Bach soon.

Johann Sebastian Bach (1685–1750)

At one time, in Northern Germany, there were musicians called Bach all over the place. Johann Sebastian was the most famous member of a huge family of singers and instrumentalists. Johann Sebastian had many jobs, such as teaching, writing and playing music for lots of the German aristocracy. Although he wrote joyful and soothing music, he occasionally flipped, himself. Once, he got so cross with an organist who'd played the wrong note that he whipped off his own wig and threw it at him. Another time, he had a punch-up in the street with one of his music students.

In-between writing lots of choir music, organ music and masses of other stuff, he found time to get married a couple of times and to have twenty children.

Track 36:
Rainbow, Traditional

This music is based on a Brazilian tune. It's a traditional tune, which means it's been around for years and nobody knows who wrote it. It's played on flute and guitar. It has a Latin American feel to it (the cabassa in the background helps that), so it has a connection to 'Mambo' in the Rhythm Room. 'Rainbow' is dreamier, though — the rhythm is very loose and relaxed.

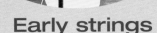

Elizabeth Neville, cello, BBC Philharmonic Orchestra

Stringed instruments

The modern violin dates from the 1500s, when it first appeared in Italy. It developed from Ancient Asian stringed instruments. The violin is the highest of the string sounds and was first used mainly to accompany singing, or in dance music. It is extremely busy in all styles of music: orchestra, folk, string quartets, and so on, nowadays.

The viola looks very similar to a violin but is slightly bigger and can play lower notes. It has a darker, richer and warmer sound than the violin, and it's more difficult to play fast. It was introduced later than the violin, in the 1700s.

The cello is even bigger than the viola. It has to be held upright between your knees rather than on your shoulder. Cellos used to vary a lot in size until the 18th Century, when instrument maker, Antonio Stradivari, decided on a standard length for adult cellists of 75 to 76cm. There are smaller versions for younger players. It has a deep, mellow sound.

The double bass is the lowest stringed instrument of all. It varies in shape and size. It has gone through several hundred years of changes in design and fashion. It's used mainly to supply power and weight to the string sound in the orchestra.

Q **What do you get if you cross a chicken with a guitar?**

A **A chicken that plays tunes when you pluck it.**

Early strings

The string instrument you can hear on Track 36, 'Rainbow' is an acoustic guitar. Acoustic means its sound isn't amplified (made louder) using electricity. Guitars have been around for centuries and developed from the oud (see page 51).

The very first sort of stringed instrument was probably dreamed up when prehistoric hunters noticed the twanging sound the string on their bow made when they pulled it back and let go to fire an arrow.

Most ancient musical bows were simply a bit of string made from animal hair or bits of plant tied to each end of a bendy stick. Some time later, a bright spark had the idea of holding a hollow wooden sound box (such as a coconut shell) against the bow. The air inside the 'box' picked up the vibrations of the string and made the twang much louder.

Some African musicians still play guitars with sound boxes made from empty oil cans and manage to make them sound better than some shop-bought ones.

Acoustic and electric

Lots of instruments have electric 'cousins' to their normal, acoustic form: the violin, guitar, drums, piano and even some wind instruments. They have an electric pick-up (a tiny microphone) which picks up the sound the instrument makes and takes it into an electric amplifier, which makes the sound louder and plays it to the audience.

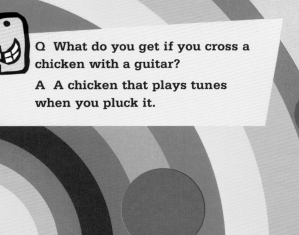

Track 37:
Theme from Star Trek, Goldsmith

Now for a dream of the future. This tune was written for the 1979 film 'Star Trek: The Motion Picture'. Jerry Goldsmith, the composer, was nominated for an Oscar for Best Original Score (see right). Star Trek is best known for being on TV. There are four different series, each with its own theme tune. The theme for the original series was written by Alexander Courage in 1966. For 'Star Trek: the Next Generation' they used Jerry Goldsmith's tune from 'The Motion Picture' again. 'Deep Space Nine' had a new theme tune by Dennis McCarthy, but Goldsmith was brought back to write the theme for the most recent series, 'Star Trek Voyager'.

Jerry Goldsmith

Jerry Goldsmith is really famous in Hollywood. Like John Williams and James Horner, who also have tracks on the CD, he has written music for loads of films. Apart from four Star Trek movies, Jerry wrote the music for all of these films which you might have heard of or seen:

'The Mummy', 'Mulan', 'Small Soldiers', 'Air Force One', 'Fierce Creatures', 'The River Wild', 'Gremlins 1 and 2', 'Total Recall', 'Lionheart', 'Innerspace' and 'The Secret of NIMH'.

Jerry comes from Los Angeles, California (Hollywood is part of Los Angeles). He started work as a typing clerk for CBS television, but it wasn't long before he was composing. His music for 'The Omen' film won him an Oscar and he's been nominated another sixteen times. He has five children who are all involved in music. His wife is a songwriter and his son, Joel, is writing film music now, too.

Score

A score is the name for written music which shows the whole of the music, not just the music for one instrument.

When people talk about a 'film score' they mean the music that goes with a film. If it is 'original', it means it's been written especially for the film. Some films use great music that already exists.

Brain teaser

An orchestra has both first and second violins. Do you know what the difference is?

The answer is – none! All big orchestras have two violin sections. The 'firsts' and 'seconds' usually play slightly different parts, or tunes, in a piece of music, and the firsts sometimes play higher notes. People often think that the 'firsts' must be better players than the 'seconds', but this isn't true. Both sets of violins can be asked to play difficult bits. Some people prefer to play second violin because they think it's more interesting.

The dream world of the movies

Music is used a lot in films and TV programmes to create an atmosphere and play on your emotions – to make you enter the dream world of the film. Films also like to have a 'big tune' as a theme tune. That's a tune you get into your head where it goes round and round, and you think of the film each time you hear it.

The CD with this book features quite a few 'big tunes' from the movies:

'Theme from Star Trek' (Track 37)

'My love goes on' (Track 41)

'The Star Wars March' (Track 50)

Other tracks have been used in films or TV, although they weren't written specially for them:

'The Sorcerer's Apprentice' (Track 21) was used in the Walt Disney film 'Fantasia' 'Mambo' (Track 3), and 'Air on a G string' (Track 35) have been used for TV commercials.

Apart from the theme tune, music's really important in helping you to enjoy the whole story of a film. For example, action and fighting make your heart race if there's some loud, stirring music and a love scene's much more romantic with a lovely tune in the background. If the composer gets this 'mood music' right, you hardly notice it's there.

When a film or TV programme has been made, the producer or director talks to the composer about the sort of music they want as background to the action. Most composers then sit down and watch and listen to the film dozens of times until they get an idea. Music written like this is called 'incidental' music and it's not normally the sort of stuff you'd sit down and listen to on its own, but you'd notice if it was missing.

Music really livens up cartoons, too. Try looking at a cartoon with the sound turned down – it isn't half as exciting. Each cartoon has its own little tunes that come back again and again. Some typical effects used are:

bell or harp sounds for anything 'magical';

two clarinets playing running notes for characters dashing around;

a sliding trombone sound if anything silly or funny happens.

Next time you watch a film or the television, try listening out specially for the music to see what atmosphere it's trying to create.

Mood words

Music's really good at creating moods. Here are some words you could use to describe different kinds of music.

Heavy, **loud,** dark, slow, firm, stepping, thundering

Busy, bustling, quick, energetic

Sparkly, light, dancing, tinkling, shimmering

Dancing, bouncy, gliding, singing, swinging

Tuneful, happy, dreamy, laughing

Spiky, smooth, hard, sharp

Creepy, spooky, eerie, strange

big, Grand, proud, royal

Bunk's dream

The American jazz trumpeter, Bunk Johnson, was once playing at a dance hall. A gangster suddenly leapt onto the stage and stabbed his trumpet-playing partner to death. In the punch-up that followed, Bunk's trumpet was ruined and his front teeth were knocked out. Now, if there's one thing you need to play a trumpet, it's your teeth.

Bunk tried tying a piece of string across the gap in his teeth to rest his mouthpiece on, but it didn't really work. In any case, he no longer had a trumpet. So poor old Bunk had to give up jazz and went to work on a farm. There, he spent his spare moments remembering his glory days and dreaming of getting some fresh teeth and a new trumpet. No-one saw him for years and years.

In the meantime, lots of other jazz musicians were busy making records and getting famous. One or two jazz fans heard of Bunk and thought it would be great if the legendary trumpeter were still around. It would be a dream come true to record his playing.

Then, one day, they found him. By now, all the rest of his teeth had fallen out! The fans didn't let this beat them. They got jazz fans from all over the place to have a whip-round and raised enough money to get Bunk some smart new teeth and a new trumpet. So their dream came true... and so did Bunk's! Even though he was quite old by this time, he made his very first records and they were terrific.

A street of jazz clubs in New Orleans, USA

ROOM FOR
Special Occasions

If something really special happens to people, such as having a special birthday, getting married, or receiving a top honour, they like to mark the occasion with a bit of a party. And, to make the party memorable, they love to have some special music playing at it.

Sometimes it's music that's been specially written for the occasion, such as the music for film and TV award ceremonies. Sometimes it's music that all sorts of people use for similar occasions, such as popular wedding tunes.

Track 39:
Fanfare from La Péri, Dukas

This brass 'fanfare' (see the next page for more about fanfares) really makes you sit up and pay attention. Paul Dukas wrote it for his ballet, 'La Péri'. It was to be played just before the main piece in order to whip everyone into a lather of excitement and anticipation.

The ballet is about a 'péri', a sort of Turkish fairy. The main character is a man called Iskender. One day he wanders into a temple and finds a péri having a nap. He's amazed to see that she's holding the flower of everlasting life, and he steals it. The péri wakes up and is very upset. The flower turns purple, which tells Iskender that it's losing its power.

The péri then does the Dance of the Péris. Iskender falls in love with her and gives her the flower back. The péri glows, turns into a flame, then floats off. Iskender realises that he cannot live forever – he has learnt his lesson.

Paul Dukas (1865-1935)

The French composer, Paul Dukas, was extra-fussy about all the music he composed. He tinkered with it for ages until he got it exactly right. If there was just one tiny bit he wasn't satisfied with, he'd chuck the whole lot in the waste paper basket and start again.

When he wasn't composing, Paul worked as a music critic and a teacher, so he didn't get round to writing a great deal of music. But he is really famous for writing 'The Sorcerer's Apprentice' (listen to part of it on Track 21).

Vain King Louis

Some people, such as Louis XIV, the 17th Century King of France, were so puffed up with their own importance that they thought almost everything they did needed special music to go with it. Louis had different musicians to perform at all sorts of events. He had twenty-five violinists to fiddle while he fed, and twenty-four more to bow and scrape when he went to one of his homes in the country or held a dance. He had a brass band to play at ceremonies and outdoor events and his own choir to make music while he worshipped. Louis would have loved the first track in the Special Occasions Room.

Fanfares

In the old days, people who wanted to be thought of as VERY IMPORTANT PEOPLE liked nothing better than to have a group of trumpets make a big row (usually ending on a really loooooooooong note) to announce their arrival at a 'do' and get everyone excited.

When a group of archaeologists broke into Tutankhamun's tomb in the 1920s, they found two trumpets. Experts thought they were at least 3000 years old. They were probably used for fanfares for the pharaohs themselves.

In 1942, a famous American composer, called Aaron Copland, wrote a piece called 'Fanfare For The Common Man'. You've probably heard this fanfare about a thousand times without knowing it because TV advertising people are always using it.

Fanfares are also used to announce the opening of great events, such as the Millennium celebrations and Olympic Games. You can even hire little fanfare bands to announce the arrival of the guests at your wedding.

Q What does the baby tuba call his dad?

A Oom Papa.

Track 40:
Denka, Traditional

This piece of music is from West Africa and is played to celebrate the birth of a baby.

The main instrument you can hear on Denka is the wooden African xylophone called a balafon (in West African countries, such as Mali and Guinea) or a marimba (in Southern African countries, such as Zimbabwe and South Africa).

No-one's quite sure when the first marimba was made, but people think that they started off quite simply. Different-length chunks of wood were laid across a hole in the ground and were then tapped with a stick.

Modern orchestral marimbas have hollow wooden or brass tubes that hang underneath the bars to make them resonate (sound louder).

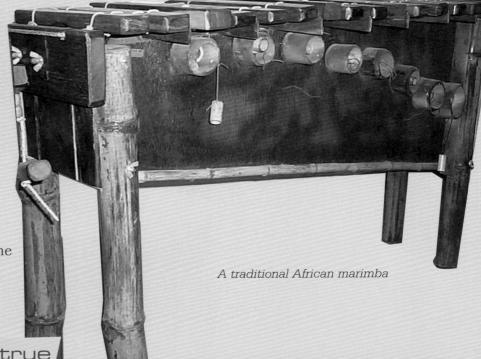

A traditional African marimba

strange, but true

Even the horses cried

Some amazing 'special occasion' music was played at funerals in the American city of New Orleans. As the coffin was taken to the cemetery on a horse-drawn carriage, it was followed by a procession of mourners and a jazz band playing slow, sad music. The moment the coffin was in the grave, the jazz band would start playing happy, jazzy tunes and the mourners would dance and sing back to town.

One of the top funeral parlours in New Orleans, Emile Labat's, went one better than anyone else. They had a hearse driver called 'Joe Never Smile' and when the band struck up its heartbreaking tunes, even his horses cried! Crafty 'Joe Never Smile' crushed onions and put the juice in a bottle. At the really sad part of the funeral, he'd tip onion juice onto his hanky and dab it under the poor horses' eyes – and great big tears would roll down their cheeks.

Track 41:
My Love Goes On, James Horner

This is music from the film, 'Titanic'. It's special occasion music because the film's about the very first time the great ship, Titanic, sailed (and about the first time it sank, too!). After the solo flute has played the main tune, the stately and heart-breaking cor anglais takes it up. Then come the other instruments in the orchestra, which all begin to create their own powerful 'waves' of sound, appropriately enough for this sea story.

The percussion brings to mind the sound of water slapping against the huge boat's hull. There's also a hint that something scary is going to happen, when the drums roll, the strings soar, the horns roar in a great swell of sound that fills you with emotion.

Guest list for the Instruments' Ball

Mr and Mrs Pani and their son, Tim

Old Pa Rimba and his wife, Ma Rimba

Mr and Mrs Nett and their daughter, Clare E.

Mr and Mrs Olin with their daughter Violet (known as Vi), and their niece, also called Vi (the second Vi Olin)

Mr and Mrs Horn and their relations from Paris, the French Horns.

Mr and Mrs Lin and their daughter, Mandy

Mr and Mrs Toe-Saxe and their son, Al

James Horner (born 1953)

James Horner was born in California, then came to London to study music. He went back to America and studied lots more, then worked hard composing classical music. After all this, his music only got played once, so he decided to write film music instead. His first movie music was for science fiction and horror films, such as 'Battle Beyond The Stars' and 'Humanoids from the Deep'. In 1982, he wrote the sound tracks for 'Star Trek II' and the cop comedy, '48 Hours', which made him famous. Since then, he's done lots more, including 'Braveheart', 'Aliens'... and, of course, 'Titanic'!

MUSIC FOR UN-SPECIAL OCCASIONS

By the way, George Owen Squier did lots of things besides inventing muzak. He was the first air passenger. He hitched a ride with Wilbur and Orville Wright on their first flight.

What have these situations got in common?

You're in a supermarket buying food

You're in a restaurant having a meal

You're on the 'phone, waiting in a call queue

You're working in a factory

Something's gone wrong with a programme on the TV

The lift's stuck and you're waiting to be let out

The answer is, you'll probably be listening to some music you didn't ask for. It's music that's supposed to calm you down or pep you up or make you want to spend money. It's called muzak. Everywhere you go these days, there's muzak playing in the background. Just listen next time you go shopping. How many of the shops have music playing?

Muzak was invented by General George Owen Squier in the USA in 1928. He found that when they played the right music to a room of army typists, they typed faster. He looked at the effect of different types of music and realised he was on to something.

Eventually, he founded the Muzak Corporation. They used to make their own recordings of pop songs, but they never sounded as good as the original. So 'muzak' also came to mean bland, boring music of any kind. Now, of course, they use the original recordings.

Muzak is exactly the opposite of Music for Special Occasions. It's music for any old time at all, especially when you're not expecting it and not listening to it.

Squier also invented multiplexing, a way of sending more than one message down a phone line at the same time — imagine the Internet without that!

50

Track 42:
2000 Celebrations, Traditional

This music comes from Egypt, where they've been playing music for thousands of years. We know this because there are paintings on the walls of ancient tombs, showing harp and lyre players. This piece is the sort of music that's played at weddings. There's always a live music knees-up at Egyptian weddings. First, a bugle and trumpet band plays – they got the idea from British Army marching bands, who were in Egypt in the days of the British Empire. The brass band is backed by a couple of dozen wooden drums, which provide a deafening beat, while everyone chants and the dancers spin. After that, a band playing the music for the belly dancer starts up (listen to Track 14 of the CD).

Nasser Shamma, a well-known Iraqui oud player

The oud

The bouncy-sounding stringed instrument you can hear on 2000 Wedding is called an oud (it rhymes with 'food'). It's an incredibly ancient instrument and may be the guitar's great, great (times 100) grandparent.

Ouds were originally used by Arab minstrels. They plucked them as they wandered around the desert reading poetry out loud. When Arab mathematicians and musicians first worked out the gaps between the notes on the musical scale, the oud was the instrument they did it on. The harpsichord family (see page 38) was used in much the same way in Europe around the 16th Century.

The word oud comes the Arabic al 'ud – which means 'the wood'. They're made from all sorts of trees, including lemons and coconuts.

When the Arabs invaded Spain in the fifteenth century, they took their ouds with them. Before too long, European instrument-makers took an interest in them and asked what they were called. When the Arabs told them, the Europeans thought they were saying 'a lute' – and that's what they called them when they made their own versions of them.

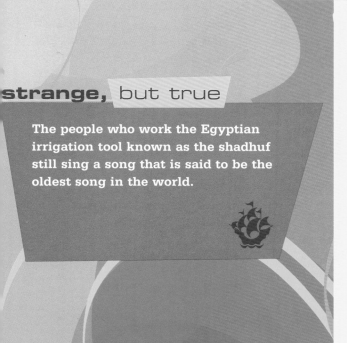

strange, but true

The people who work the Egyptian irrigation tool known as the shadhuf still sing a song that is said to be the oldest song in the world.

Q What's a burglar's favourite instrument?
A The lute.

51

Track 43:
The Defeat of Napoleon, Kodály

This music is from an opera about a legendary Hungarian folk hero, called Háry János (say Harry Yan-osh). He had a big mouth and an even bigger imagination. The music describes how Háry brags to his mates about fighting in the wars against Napoleon. He claimed he'd rescued the daughter of an important man and been made a general for his bravery. Then he'd beaten Napoleon single-handedly. Háry's friends nod and smile, but are really thinking ... 'as if!'. Háry says that

Napoleon's wife was so impressed by him that he could have married her if he'd wanted to. But, being a loyal Hungarian, he's come back to his village to marry his sweetheart.

Track 43 is the moment when Háry's bragging about bashing Napoleon. The trombones boast and bluster for him, the drums bash and the rest of the brass section trumpet the news of his 'triumph'. Listen out for a massive cymbal crash near the end of this piece.

Viola

Robert Holliday, trombone

Did you know that you have to wait until your arms are long enough before you can play the bottom notes on the trombone? Robert Holliday of the BBC Philharmonic took up the trombone when he was nine. At first, he couldn't push the slide far enough to reach those low notes, but it didn't put him off. It takes a long time to learn exactly where to push the slide for each position.

The trombone is very difficult to play quietly, but good players can use it to play beautiful tunes or melodies.

Zoltán Kodály (1882-1967)

Zoltán Kodály (pronounce it cod-eye) was born in the Hungarian countryside. Both his parents played instruments. Zoltán taught himself to play the piano, violin and viola and cello. In the evenings, the little family and their neighbours liked nothing better than to gather together and play music.

Cello

One day they wanted to play a quartet by Joseph Haydn, but the music for the cello part was missing. So Zoltán sat down and worked out what the cello bit would have sounded like and wrote it all down. Not long afterwards, his dad got another copy of the score with the cello part in it and found that Zoltán had more or less got it right!

Zoltán went off to study music and met Béla Bartók, who became his best friend (and was a famous composer too). They were both really keen on folk music. They started collecting it, which wasn't easy as folk musicians hardly ever wrote their music down. Zoltán and Béla wandered around the countryside, getting villagers to sing into their new-fangled recording machine.

Track 44:

Procession of Joy Dave Cooke

Processions are when lots of people have to walk along together in a formal line, quite often to music. This tune is played on the soprano saxophone, the smallest instrument in the sax family. The music was originally written for a Christmas play. It has also been used for a bride to walk down the aisle to at her wedding.

Dave Cooke, born 1952

Dave started playing the piano at an early age and taught himself guitar from the age of 11. He is also trained on the double bass and percussion. He started writing and composing small films for TV and audio visual presentations. Now he has his own recording facility in West London and does a variety of projects, including music albums, music for TV programmes, including Blue Peter, and special Internet projects.

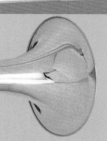

Q How much do trombone lessons cost?
A Well, they're on a sliding scale.

Do-it-yourself special occasion

With a friend (or several), decide on a special occasion you'd like to attend: the wedding of someone famous; a special birthday or a royal event, for example. Pick some special occasion music from the CD, dress up as grandly or outrageously as you like and decide how you will use the music: is it playing as the guests arrive, as they queue to meet the famous person, or as you hand over gifts? Think about how the grand clothes and special music make you feel.

SURPRISE ROOM

'A well-known music writer, called Whitney Balliett, once wrote that jazz music was 'the sound of surprise'. The famous conductor, Sir Thomas Beecham, said that the best music is the sort that surprises you, then leaves you 'with feelings of wonder and contentment'…

Music that surprises listeners sometimes gives the people who make it a surprise too. A great new musical thought suddenly comes to them and they're thrilled because it's theirs and completely new and original. So they steam ahead with their playing or writing because they don't know what's around the next musical corner. It could be something even better.

Hearing new music is a similar experience because you don't know what's coming next. With really great music, even though you may have heard it tons of times before, some bits still manage to be as surprising and satisfying as the first time you heard them.

Track 46: Toy Symphony, Leopold Mozart

 During the 18th Century, there was a little place called Berchtesgaden, which is now in Austria. It was famous for the pretty wooden instruments that they made there. Many of these were tiny toy instruments on which you could actually play proper music.

Completely normal-sized composers wrote special little pieces of music for these tiny instruments. They were known as 'Berchtesgaden Symphonies'. When Leopold's soon-to-be-famous son (Wolfgang Amadeus – see the section about the composer, on the right) was small, he liked to stomp about tooting his tiny trumpet or tweeting his mini-flute. It's said that this gave Leopold the idea of writing the 'Toy Symphony'.

He wrote it just before 1760, but some time afterwards it was lost. It didn't turn up again until 1941. Musicologists spend ages arguing about who really did write the 'Toy Symphony'. One group reckons it was Leopold, but another lot say it was Franz Joseph Haydn. They are still squabbling about it.

Leopold Mozart (1719-1787)

Leopold Mozart was a talented composer and violinist who lived in Austria in the 18th Century. He was also a musical theorist, which means he wrote loads of stuff about music that most of us probably couldn't make head or tail of.

In 1763, the Prince Archbishop of Salzburg (yes, in those days you could be a prince and an archbishop) gave Leopold the job of being deputy Kappelmeister at his court. This meant that he was second in charge of the Prince Archbishop's orchestra. In 1747, Leopold got married and then had seven children. Sadly, five of them died, leaving just one girl and a little boy, whom they called Wolfgang Amadeus.

By the time he was four, little Wolfgang was playing the piano brilliantly. By the time he was six, he was giving concerts and composing music. Leopold realised that his little lad had amazing talent and that they should make the most of it. He took Wolfgang all over Europe to play his music in front of the rich and powerful.

Sadly, when Wolfgang grew up and got married, he and Leopold had a bit of a tiff about his new bride and they never really made up the quarrel again. Leopold got depressed and died a bit later. As well as writing the 'Toy Symphony' (or not, as the case may be – see the story on the left), Leopold also wrote the 'Hunting Symphony'. This featured four hunting horns and a shotgun that was fired throughout the piece at set moments.

Rumon Gamba

Rumon Gamba, conductor

Rumon Gamba is one of the conductors for the BBC Philharmonic Orchestra. He says his work begins when he's asked to conduct a piece of music. He has to sit down and study the score very carefully until he knows the music in his head from beginning to end. The musicians only have to learn their own parts. Rumon says you need to know the music very well, so that when you are with the orchestra, you can explain to them exactly how you would like them to play.

Next, the conductor rehearses with the orchestra. They go over the difficult bits and make sure that everyone knows when to come in. A rehearsal may take an hour or so, or, if it's a new or difficult work, it can take all week.

He says it is just as important for a conductor to learn as many instruments as possible and to play in an orchestra. You can learn how to beat time, and some of the simple things, yourself. But, to become a proper conductor, you need a good teacher.

Are we nearly there yet, dad? **Almost, son. Just time for you to write another symphony.**

Track 47:
Czervony Pas, Traditional

This is a folk song from South-Eastern Poland.
The title means 'red is the belt'.
The words, written nearly 200 years ago, are all about gleaming hatchets and courage and what fun it is to live in the hills.

Dancing was very popular with Polish villagers. They often began their dances very slowly, but would then speed up.

Some dances gave young Polish lads the chance to show off to the local girls.

In one dance, a full cup of wine is put in the middle of the room. Dancers take turns to dash forward, pick up the cup with their teeth, drink all the wine, then hurl the cup backwards over their heads – all with no hands and without spilling a drop of wine. In another dance, the lads light a fire in the middle of the dance floor and take turns to leap over it.

strange, but true

A surprise comeback

A top opera star was once playing the lead part in 'Tosca', an opera by Giacomo Puccini (1858 -1942). She was a great singer but she wasn't all that popular with the stage hands and everyone who worked behind the scenes.

Towards the end of the opera, the tragic heroine throws herself off a castle wall and plunges to her doom hundreds of feet below. Of course, on stage, all the star really does is fling herself off a pretend wall and drop a few feet onto a mattress hidden behind it. However, to the audience, it does look as if she's slung herself to her death.

On this occasion, the star stood on the castle ramparts, sang her final tragic words, and hurled herself to her 'death'. A moment later, she shot back up above the castle wall. Then she disappeared again... and reappeared... the backstage hands had mischievously replaced her mattress with a trampoline.

Brain teaser

Music has been recorded in lots of different ways over the last century – on vinyl records, tapes and CDs for example. Do you know what kind of recordings these initials stand for?

CD   LP   MC   MD   MP3   DVD

Answers: CD – compact disc; LP – long player (vinyl record); MC – musicassette; MD – mini disc; MP3 – MPEG-3, which stands for Motion Picture Experts' Group Layer 3; DVD – Digital Versatile Disc.

Big is beautiful

Remember Johann Strauss from the Rhythm Room (see page 9)? Well, in 1872 his son, also called Johann, conducted an orchestra with **987** musicians in it. This was in Boston, Massachusetts, at a big 'do' called the World Peace Jubilee. The choir had **2000** people in it.

In 1991, youth orchestras from Mexico, Venezuela and the former Soviet Union got together to make an orchestra with **2000** players. They gave a concert in Mexico City.

Those giant orchestras are just lots of people playing music that was actually written for a normal-sized orchestra. The biggest number of people actually needed to play some things can also be huge, though. British composer, Havergal Brian, wrote his 'Gothic Symphony' in 1927. It needs a symphony orchestra with **160** players (**10** in the percussion section), **4** brass bands, a large choir, a children's choir and four solo singers. The piece is also nearly two hours long; it's the longest symphony ever written. It is so expensive to perform that it wasn't actually played until 1966. In 1980, it was performed with a chorus of **850** singers, meaning the total number of performers was well over **1000**. There wasn't a lot of room left in the Royal Albert Hall for the audience!

Guatav Mahler's 'Symphony No. 8, Symphony of a Thousand', is pretty big, too. The **1000** is just the choir – it needs a huge orchestra on top of that.

Track 48:
East Street Arcadia, Bill Connor

The surprise in this piece is that it has a couple of tunes in it you might have heard somewhere before. They're signature tunes from 'soaps' and should be easy to spot. However, clever Mr Connor has sneaked a few other things in there, too: not just tunes, but styles, too.

See if you can hear some of the surprises – look at the Brain teaser on this page to find out more.

Bill Connor

Did you think all composers were dead? Bill Connors certainly isn't. He says that the 'tools' you need to be a composer are the sounds in your head, not dots on a page. Writing down your music just helps tell other people what to play and how to play it.

Bill was brought up in the East End of London. He can remember playing tunes with one finger on the piano at Primary school. Later, he taught himself guitar and bass guitar, and tried to learn the piano, too. He was interested in all sorts of music, including rock.

He didn't suddenly 'decide' to become a composer — he says it 'chose' him. In the 1960s, to copyright, or 'own', a piece of music, it had to be written down. Bill got the job of writing down music for rock musicians.

These days, most of his work begins when someone contacts him and asks him to write something. He starts composing outlines, a bit like a painter makes a sketch. Then he 'colours' it with sounds. He may add a 'bright' sound, like a trumpet, or the 'mellow' sound of some French horns. That's called orchestration – which is really just painting with sounds.

Brain teaser

You'll hear some interesting things in 'East Street Arcadia' if you listen closely. The challenge is to find five hidden things.

There are two 'soap' theme tunes, the music from an old film and two classical music references, at least. The last three are more tricky to spot, but you should be able to hear the 'soaps'. You could ask some adults if they've got any ideas about the others.

Answers:
Soap theme: EastEnders
Soap theme: Coronation Street
Movie theme: Gone with the Wind
Classical theme: Elgar, Enigma Variations no. 8
Hidden style: Tchaikovsky, 'Dance of the Reed Pipes' from 'Nutcracker Suite'

58

The earliest thing that was like an orchestra was the medieval mixed consort of around the 15th Century. This would have used a few old-style wind instruments: recorders, crumhorns, sackbuts (see page 25); and some old stringed instruments called viols, with maybe some percussion and a lute thrown in.

The full orchestra

In the 17th and 18th Centuries, the baroque orchestra used modern violins, violas, cellos and double basses. They had a few of each instrument playing each part to make a bigger sound. Wind instruments included a flute or recorder, one or two oboes, a bassoon, trumpets and horns. They usually kept together by having a harpsichord player.

A hundred years later, the classical orchestra wasn't a lot different to the Baroque orchestra, except that they made the string section even bigger. They also started to add trombones and new-fangled instruments, like the clarinet. They normally had two of each wind instrument. They almost always had a pair of timpani (kettledrums). The harpsichord player was replaced by a conductor. His job was to make sure everyone played at the right time.

The modern orchestra developed in the middle of the 19th Century and just kept getting bigger and bigger. Composers used three or four of each wind instrument. They wanted all the extras, such as the piccolo, cor anglais, bass clarinet and contrabassoon. The bass trombone and tuba also got in on the act. The string sections were huge to balance all the rest, and made a very rich sound. There was a proper percussion section, with several players, one or two harps and, sometimes, a piano and celesta (a small keyboard instrument). Now composers really had the 'full works' to write for.

In the 21st Century, there are still a few changes. The percussion has become a fully-developed section of the orchestra. You might also find newer instruments, such as saxophones, an electric violin, synthesizers and guitars. Sometimes, electronic processors alter the music 'live', as it's being made. The orchestra might even play alongside a tape of electronic sounds or a video.

To keep a big orchestra going today, you need lots of other people apart from the musicians. Look at all these jobs that have to be done:

- ☆ Arranging rehearsals and concerts
- ☆ Booking transport, food and accommodation
- ☆ Advertising and promoting the orchestra
- ☆ Buying or hiring music for them to play
- ☆ Looking after the finances
- ☆ Arranging recordings

Track 49:
Funky Dhol,
Kuljit Bhamra

'Funky Dhol' is Kuljit Bhamra's stunning mix of modern techno-pop and traditional Indian music, called Bhangra. Bhangra started off as folk dance music that was played in the Punjab in Northern India (see Dance Room page 21). The main instrument used back then was a big, wooden, barrel-shaped drum, called a dhol. It was hit with a stick, while people chanted, swished their scythes and clapped their hands.

Since then, Bhangra has bounced into the high-tech 21st Century with a bang, a touch of techno and synthesizer, some sampling and a helping of hip hop, rap and reggae. It's massively popular and you can hear it now in the UK charts, at discos, wedding parties ... and on the Blue Peter CD.

Musician playing a dhol

Kuljit Bhamra

Kuljit is an award-winning composer, a brilliant drummer and a record producer. When he's not making his own records or doing live gigs, he works in his recording studio in London, helping up-and-coming Bhangra stars take-off on the music scene.

He wrote the music for the award-winning Channel Four movie, 'Bhaji On the Beach'; played his drums on the soundtracks of 'A Little Princess' and 'Wings of a Dove'; and has won lots of awards for his Bhangra music.

Kuljit likes all sorts of music. His favourite things include Soul, Prince, old sci-fi movie music, Garage, Stevie Wonder and Bollywood sound tracks (Indian film music). He has recently worked on records with Ringo Starr, of the Beatles, and the jazz saxophonist, Andy Sheppard.

Dhols

Dhols are made from a large, wooden shell with goat skins stretched over each end. Rope is woven through the edge of the skins so you can tighten or slacken them to produce high or low sounds.

Dhols were used to spur on warriors in Mogul times in India, and also to announce a messenger with news. Drum sounds are still widely used these days to grab your attention. Think of drum rolls to announce that someone is arriving or that something is about to happen.

Brain teaser

Which word actually means 'empty orchestra' in Japanese, but is used to mean singing along to a backing track?

Answer: Karaoke.

Track 50: Star Wars March, John Williams

'A long time ago in a galaxy far, far away…' This fabulous piece finishes off the CD. John Williams wrote it in 1977 when the first Star Wars movie (Episode IV) was released. Science-fiction movies in the 1960s and '70s tended to have weird, electronic soundtracks. The big, romantic orchestral sound was very unusual then.

On the track, you can hear a surprising range of different moods and styles. There's Luke Skywalker's theme (heroic), Princess Leia's theme (tender), and lots of juicy extra bits that link some of the best sequences in the film together. 'May the Force be with you', music lovers!

John Williams

John Williams has composed and directed the music for nearly eighty great modern films. These include successful 'blockbusters' that you may have seen, such as 'Jurassic Park', 'Indiana Jones and the Temple of Doom', 'Jaws', 'Raiders of the Lost Ark', 'The Empire Strikes Back', 'Star Wars' and 'E.T. (The Extra-Terrestrial)'.

John was born in New York. After studying music, he joined the American Air Force for a while, and played jazz piano in clubs and on records. After that, he got a job in some music studios and, in the 1960s, he began writing theme music for TV programmes. John also composes and conducts symphonies and concertos and has made lots of best-selling albums. As well as all this, John was the conductor of the Boston Pops Orchestra from 1980–83. He has received stacks of honours for his musical achievements.

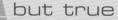

stranger but true

John Williams' 'Star Wars' sound track album sold more than four million copies. It's the best selling, non-pop, long-playing record ever.

61

Index